W9-AZG-395

MANET

MANET

Sarah Carr-Gomm

STUDIO EDITIONS

LONDON

To my Mother and Father

Published in Great Britain by
Studio Editions Ltd
Princess House
50 Eastcastle Street
London W1N 7AP

Copyright © 1992 Studio Editions Ltd

The right of Sarah Carr-Gomm to be identified
as the author of this work has been asserted
by her in accordance with the Copyright, Designs
and Patents Act, 1988.

All rights reserved. No part of this publication
may be reproduced, stored in a retrieval system,
or transmitted, in any form or by any means, electronic,
mechanical, photocopying, recording or otherwise,
without the prior permission of the copyright holder.

ISBN 1 85170 823 5

Printed and bound in Hong Kong

INTRODUCTION

'He is a man of our age' the novelist Emile Zola wrote of Manet in 1867. This was intended as the highest compliment; progressive thinkers of the mid-nineteenth century regarded 'modernity' as an essential ingredient for an artist of merit. What Zola saw was a man of great individuality with an intuitive and honest response to the modern world. Manet had an inexhaustible interest in the advances of his age. His awareness of new fashions, scientific discoveries, current events, contemporary literature and artistic developments gave his work a vitality and diversity unparalleled in nineteenth-century painting. But Manet's paintings are not merely a record of his era, nor are they a superficial illustration of transient fashions. His observations are applicable to any age regardless of the accessories and details which fix them in time.

Although Manet died when he was only fifty-one he left a considerable volume of work which illustrates the great range of his subject matter and style. Primarily a painter of human figures (although he also produced still lifes), Manet's *œuvre* includes religious subjects, genre, landscapes, contemporary events, seascapes and animal subjects. He worked on large-scale canvases and also made tiny sketches. Some paintings are profoundly serious yet others are light-hearted. 'It has always been my ambition not to equal myself, not to repeat tomorrow what I did yesterday, but to inspire myself constantly with new aspects, to search to make a new note heard' he said. Manet tackled new ideas and styles which outraged the reactionaries who despaired for the state of art to come. His painting was unappreciated by the critics and they established him as a highly controversial figure. Whenever he exhibited his work attracted attention, most of which was hostile. But even under a barrage of criticism, Manet's determination to succeed never weakened. Undaunted, he claimed, 'I have suffered cruelly, but it drives me on'.

Although Manet was branded as a revolutionary, there are ways in which he was a traditionalist. Throughout his life he firmly believed that the only valid form of recognition was through the official channels. In many ways, his strength came from a traditional respect for the achievements of his predecessors. Some of Manet's greatest works are modern interpretations of paintings by old masters. The works of the past provided him not only with inspiration but also with a standard of excellence to which he could aspire.

Manet's work defies art historical classification. He always sought to remain independent but nevertheless the Establishment labelled him a 'Realist' and an 'Impressionist' and considered him to be the leader of the avant-garde. Although he did not wish to be categorized with a group of painters, he was a loyal friend to the Impressionists and his integrity and strength of personality encouraged them to pursue their convictions. His work was of vital importance for his contemporaries and for his successors.

Edouard Manet was born in Paris on 26 January 1832. He came from a respected, well-to-do family and he inherited the social graces of his class. His father's family had been wealthy landowners and magistrates for several generations and August Manet was himself a high official, Head of Department at the Ministry of Justice. On his mother's side, there were distinguished diplomats and army officers; she was the daughter of an emissary to Stockholm and god-daughter of Marshal Bernadotte, later King Charles XIV of Sweden.

Manet's father wanted him to follow a professional career, one suitable for a member of the *haute bourgeoisie*. Manet chose the Navy, failed his entrance exams and subsequently went to sea as an apprentice cadet. He was finally rejected by the Navy after a voyage to Rio de Janeiro, presumably due more to his lack of interest than ability. He wrote home from sea, 'It seems to me I've been on board for months; a sailor's life is so boring! Nothing but sea and sky.' Apparently, at school his passion for drawing led him to neglect all other lessons and often on Sundays he went to look at paintings in the Louvre with his uncle, who encouraged his interest. In 1849 his father grudgingly consented to his studying art.

In order to embark on a successful career as a painter, Manet was expected to follow the official system of his day. The Académie des Beaux-Arts was originally founded by Louis XIV in order to control the development and production of art. After the Revolution it was still bound to the State and held the official monopoly on questions of aesthetic taste. Any opposition to its doctrine was seen as political criticism. Works most highly favoured by the Academy were known as 'History Painting', which drew on classical styles and depicted subjects from antiquity or the Bible, paintings with noble forms and moral messages. With the social upheavals occurring in the nineteenth century, many felt that this was an inappropriate attitude for the modern age.

Painters studied at the Ecole des Beaux-Arts where the teachers were appointed by the members of the

Academy. Students were subjected to a series of competitions and the Academicians sanctioned the prizes. The most important was the Prix de Rome, and the higher accolades carried substantial prize-money. Manet chose to study under Thomas Couture and he must have valued the instruction, as he stayed in Couture's studio for six years. Couture did not force his pupils to be candidates for the Prix de Rome; in fact, none of Couture's pupils ever won. Manet agreed, 'We are not interested in Rome and we don't want to go there. We are in Paris and let us stay here'. Manet was happiest when he was in Paris. 'It is not possible to live anywhere else' he said. Throughout his life the city was being radically transformed both physically and socially and in these exciting modern developments Manet found a rich source of inspiration. Few of his paintings, however, depict the new city of Paris itself; his interest lay in the people who populated it.

In the mid-nineteenth century, the oldest parts of Paris were delapidated slums; the squalid, over-crowded, narrow, medieval streets were difficult to negotiate, the sewage system was a threat to public health and there was little street lighting. Paris urgently needed modernizing. The problems were exacerbated by the ever-increasing population which more than doubled in size in Manet's lifetime. Even before he became Emperor in 1851, Napoleon III had grandiose plans for Paris. Under Baron Haussmann, Prefect of the Department of the Seine, slums in the central and eastern parts north of the river were demolished. They were replaced with fifty kilometres of streets which linked quarters and gave easy access to the expanding railway stations. Haussmann built magnificent broad boulevards, public gardens, railway stations, modern markets, cafés, theatres, operas and race tracks. Napoleon III intended Paris to be a

The Absinthe Drinker. *1858–59.*
Oil on canvas, 117.5 × 103 cm
NY Carlsberg Glyptotek, Copenhagen

model city and the cultural centre of Europe. In order to further his desire he organized great World's Fairs in 1855 and 1867. Napoleon's new Paris was for the financially successful classes he supported, for the affluent bourgeois, the entrepreneur, the owners of department stores, banks, hotels and large apartment blocks.

Baron Haussmann's remodelling of Paris forms much of the city we know today but when the project began enormous social problems were revealed. The massive demolition works evicted many of the working classes and exposed the vast extremes of wealth and poverty. The latter Manet chose to make the subject of his first major painting, *The Absinthe Drinker* (see page 7). Zola's novels describe those in the lowest-paid forms of employment, for example laundresses, who turned to drink to survive their wretched conditions and long working days, which could last up to eighteen hours; they spent above their income and many had to resort to prostitution. This was an embarrassing issue for the Establishment and one which Manet also confronted in *Olympia* and *Nana* (pages 67 and 119). The expanding city created a feeling of loss of identity, of anonymity in a rapidly changing world. A new class emerged, neither working class nor bourgeois, of clerks and shop-girls; they appeared to be enjoying the city but underneath their superficial gaiety there often lay loneliness and anxiety.

Thus the new city of Paris was as frightening to some as it was exciting to others. Many of its inhabitants felt uneasy about the changes. An entry in the Goncourt brothers' journal of November 1860 expresses these misgivings:

Our Paris, the Paris in which we were born, the Paris of the manners of 1830 to 1848, is disappearing. And it is not disappearing materially but morally. Social life is beginning to undergo a great change. . . . Life is threatening to become public. The club for the upper classes, the café for the lower – this is what society and the common people are coming to. All this makes me feel like a traveller in this my

spiritual homeland . . . It is silly to come into the world in a time of change; the soul feels as uncomfortable as a man who moves into a new house before the plaster is dry.

Manet never felt this unease and it was in the café that he made some of his most acute observations of everyday life. Manet was known as a *flaneur* and a *boulevardier*, a sophisticated Parisian who liked to walk the new boulevards and sit in cafés. His studios were chosen for their situation in fashionable areas which attracted a remarkable number of artists, writers and theatre people, and which contained newspaper offices, music halls, opera houses and cafés of every variety.

Just as there were differing attitudes to the changes in Paris, there was also a mid-century reassessment of the traditional values of art. Contradictions and confusion followed. The dominant figures of the painters Jean Auguste Dominique Ingres and Eugène Delacroix had fostered aesthetic and political debate because of their opposite interests; Classical versus Romantic, line versus colour and the idealized versus the naturalistic. Of these two great figures, Manet respected the painterly qualities of Delacroix's work. As a student, he had visited the master's studio to ask for permission to copy his *Dante and Virgil*. Couture's fame, on the other hand, rested chiefly on a massive painting of a classical orgy, *Les Romains de la decadence* of 1847, although the prospectus to his studio advocated that he

opposes the spurious classical school which reproduces the works of bygone times in a banal and imperfect fashion. He is even more hostile to that abominable school known under the rubric of 'Romantic' and views with disfavour the tendencies towards petty commercialism of art.

Thomas Couture was one of the more liberal masters. Although he had trained in the classical tradition his work demonstrates strong tonal contrasts and a freedom of handling which were to influence Manet. He would also encourage his students to record spon-

Study for a Portrait of Edouard Manet. *c.1864.*
Edgar Degas. Black chalk, 32.5 × 22.8 cm
The Metropolitan Museum of Art, New York

ated Manet by assuming an heroic stance thrusting out his chest and flexing his muscles. Manet shouted 'What! Can't you be natural? Do you stand like that when you go to buy a bunch of radishes at the greengrocers?'

Although Manet disagreed fundamentally with some of the doctrines of the Academy, he always hoped for public approval through the official system. An artist's work was judged at the exhibition of the Academy known as the Salon (it was originally held in the Salon Carré in the Louvre). This venue inevitably associated the exhibits on display with the masterpieces in the Louvre and reinforced the Academy's emulation of the old masters. Manet also had a profound respect for the masterpieces in the museums and he presented his paintings year after year to the Salon jury for acceptance. The jury was an élite group of officially appointed men and their decisions often caused controversy: they could, for example, join forces and refuse to accept any potential troublemaker who might challenge the Establishment. To be accepted by the jury was more than just a question of pride; exhibiting in the Salon was the most effective way of finding a buyer and consequently of continuing one's career as a painter.

Mid-nineteenth-century Salons were major social events. They exhibited over 5,000 paintings which were seen by 10,000 paying visitors each day. Journalists discussed the exhibition at length in the newspapers and the influence of the critics was enormous. A pocket-companion was printed for spectators which told them what to look at and with what attitude, and how to comment on what they saw. How the painting was hung on the overcrowded walls determined whether or not it could be seen. During the exhibition public approval could mean that popular paintings were rehung more favourably. Various methods of improving the hanging were tried without much success; in 1861 the works were hung in alphabetical order which resulted in some extraordinary juxtapositions.

taneous images, men on scaffolding or a locomotive, and to draw quick sketches of people in the streets. There are reports that Manet frustrated his master who thought that his pupil was a mere caricaturist: 'my poor boy, you will never be anything more than the Daumier of your day'. Manet, on the other hand, is reported to have said, 'I can't think why I'm here, everything we see here is absurd; the light's false, the shadows are false. When I arrive at the studio I feel as though I'm entering a tomb'. Couture's models took up traditional poses: one, named Donato, exasper-

Although the Academy primarily revered the works of Raphael and antiquity, artistic taste was broadening. They also admired the Venetian, Spanish and Dutch schools and paintings inspired by them were readily accepted by the Salon jury. While Manet was in Couture's studio in the early 1850s he travelled to the Hague, Amsterdam, Dresden, Munich and Vienna, and then to Florence, Rome and Venice to study the works of the artists he admired. He worked on several canvases which paraphrase various masterpieces and made copies of paintings by Titian, Tintoretto, Veláz-quez and Goya. Manet's *The Spanish Singer* and *Le Bon Bock* (pages 45 and 103) were virtually the only works to find praise among the critics because they derive directly from Spanish and Dutch art. However, when he exhibited *Le déjeuner sur l'herbe* and *Olympia*, which were inspired by masterpieces of the Venetian school but reinterpreted to express the values of his own age, he received only derision (pages 65 and 67).

Nevertheless, the popularity of History Painting, the favoured subject matter of the traditionalists, was slowly diminishing. The bureaucratic class of the Second Empire had very different artistic tastes to those of the more erudite patrons of the earlier part of the century. Old themes were losing their meaning. Many among the increasing number of people who visited the Salon had little biblical or classical education. They were not interested in the long explanations of the exhibits given in the catalogues and would rather look at paintings depicting contemporary events or anecdotal scenes. The number of portraits and still lifes selected remained constant but landscape and genre painting became increasingly popular, especially pictures of the typical activities of individuals such as gypsies, peasants, fishermen, orphans and beggars. These paintings did not moralize and were treated with charm and sentimentality in order to appeal to a wider, less educated audience. Traditionalists were in despair and claimed that both artists and public had no education, no religion, no interest in the past and, worst of all, no 'moral sense'.

The Government confirmed the view that contemporary art was depraved when in 1869 it offered the massive prize of 100,000 francs to raise the level of art. Reactionaries and revolutionaries alike agreed that art was in a poor state. In 1853 Théophile Gautier stated 'Today art has at its disposal only dead ideas and formulae which no longer correspond to its needs . . . It is well known that something must be done but what?'

For Manet, Gustave Courbet was the main example of an artist who had decided to defy the official system. Courbet had no interest in the sentimental and had championed the cause of 'Realism'. In 1855, to coincide with the first World's Fair, he erected a space to exhibit his works which he called his *Pavillon du Réalisme*. He claimed 'Painting is an art of sight and should therefore eschew both the historical scenes of the classical school and poetic subjects chosen from Goethe and Shakespeare of the kind chosen by the Romantics'. Courbet wanted to 'translate the habits, the ideas, the aspects of my epoch according to my understanding, to be a man as well as a painter, in a word, to make living art'. For his painting of *The Stone Breaker*, the lowest form of labour, he was deemed a revolutionary and a socialist. His political activities were to lead to brief imprisonment and voluntary exile at the end of his life. Manet agreed with Courbet's view that classical subjects and sentimental interpretations were irrelevant to their age but he had no desire to become a revolutionary figurehead.

For the Salon of 1859, Manet submitted his first large canvas, *The Absinthe Drinker* (see page 7). Although he had left Couture's studio in 1856 he still took paintings back to his former teacher for comment. When Couture saw *The Absinthe Drinker* he was reported to have said that he thought it was Manet who had drunk too much absinthe. The painting was rejected, apparently against the advice of Delacroix who was the only member of the jury to speak in its favour.

Manet said of *The Absinthe Drinker* 'I did . . . a Parisian character whom I had studied and, in executing it, I put in the simplicity of technique that I see in Velázquez's work'. It was partly the technique which upset the traditionalists. They criticized the absence of pictorial space and they thought that the application of the paint was crude. The image itself was also found offensive. Baron Haussmann had intended to glamorize the Empire but ironically, by modernizing Paris, he exposed its enormous poverty. Manet painted, without sentiment, one of the vagrants who inhabited the area around the Louvre. Zola described this ragpicker as a 'miserable and apathetic man, downtrodden by life'. The dark palette and the figure's awkward stance, unheroic in the extreme, emphasize his position as a drifter with no social standing in the new metropolis.

Manet must have been undeterred by the adverse criticism he received as he included *The Absinthe Drinker* as one of the miscellaneous figures in *The Old Musician*, painted some three years later (page 51). The failure of *The Absinthe Drinker* prompted him to say 'People don't understand. Perhaps they will understand better if I do a Spanish character'. In nineteenth-century France, Spain held a particular fascination. Hispanicism had been popular with writers, painters and poets since the end of the 1830s. King Louis-Philippe had had designs on the Spanish throne and encouraged an interest in that school of art. In 1838 the Spanish gallery was opened in the Louvre, exhibiting numerous works by Velázquez, Goya, and Murillo. At the monarch's downfall in 1850 the collection was sold but Manet must have remembered it from his Sunday visits to the Louvre. In 1853 Napoleon III married Eugénie, a Spanish beauty, and she brought Spanish fashions to Paris. Musicians, especially guitarists, and other entertainers were highly popular and during the 1860s bullfights were held in Paris. Many would have felt the tragedy of the dispersal of the Spanish collection but in 1858 the Louvre began to replace it and bought at auction works by Velázquez, Zurbaran and Ribera.

A painting of a Spanish guitarist was, therefore, more likely to find favour than one of a ragpicker. Again Manet chose to depict a poor man, an itinerant musician but he guessed that, dressed as a costume piece, the picture might even be successful. *The Spanish Singer* (page 45) was not only accepted by the Salon jury but also received praise from both the critics and the public who demanded that it be rehung more advantageously. Encouraged by this success, Manet painted numerous Spanish themes during the early 1860s. He went to see Mariano Camprubi's troupe of Spanish dancers when they arrived in 1862 and he invited the performers, most notably Lola de Valence, to pose for him in his studio. He bought Spanish clothes, which he loved for their bright colours, and dressed his models in them for his compositions. Manet did not actually visit Spain until 1865 and then only for ten days. He spent the time mostly in Madrid where he admired Velázquez 'who alone is worth the whole journey'. Manet's fascination with Spain was evident at an 1867 exhibition at Martinet's Gallery, where twenty-eight of the fifty-three works on show were of Spanish themes or models. At the end of the Salon of 1861, *The Spanish Singer* won an honourable mention and it was many years before Manet received such public acclaim again. The painting attracted the attention of a group of artists and critics including Henri Fantin-Latour, Alphonse Legros, Félix Bracquemond, Jules Champfleury and Edmond Duranty who visited Manet's studio to express their admiration.

Manet had established himself in a studio at 81 rue Guyot where friends and admirers would come and call. Alternatively, he could be found early in the evening at the fashionable Café Tortoni. An idea of Manet's personality can be gained from anecdotes told by his friends and acquaintances. Most often cited are the reminiscences of Antonin Proust, his lifelong friend, whose *Souvenirs* were published in 1913. Manet himself wrote relatively little as he thought that each artist should stick to his own profession. His few existing letters only reinforce other accounts. Manet had a forceful character and it is not surprising to find some contradictions, but most agree that he was extremely generous, had great personal charm and enjoyed stimulating company. Emile Zola, art critic, author and one of Manet's close friends, wrote 'he confessed to me that he adored society and discovered secret pleasures in the perfumed and brilliant delights of evening parties'.

Manet was intelligent and single-minded. Friends admired the frank passion of his convictions. He was decisive and spoke in simple, clear-cut phrases. He could also be impetuous. The journalist Armand Silvestre wrote 'he was naturally ironical in his conversation and frequently cruel. He had an inclination for punches, cutting and slashing with a single blow. But how striking were his expressions and often how just his observations!' Above all, however, Manet was a gentleman. Proust recalled that 'even when he tried . . . he could never succeed in being vulgar'. Many descriptions of Manet comment on the scrupulous way in which he dressed. He could be seen in elegantly-cut clothing with a tall silk hat, gold chain in his vest and a walking stick in his gloved hands, a costume, we are told, he always wore, in the country as well as the city.

During the 1860s Manet's closest companion was Charles Baudelaire, whom he had met in 1859. Baudelaire was a highly intelligent and perceptive mid-nineteenth century Bohemian who overindulged in opium and alcohol. Outraged at his recklessness, his step-father had sent him on a sea voyage to India. This only served to further his taste for the exotic and on his return home he took a coloured mistress (page 53). He greatly admired Delacroix and found a 'twin soul' in Edgar Allan Poe. In 1857 his book of poems *Les Fleurs du mal* scandalized the middle classes who thought it was deliberately designed to offend them. Baudelaire was a failed suicide and was surrounded by debts. Critics have connected his socialist attitude and melancholy and dissolute life with the abject figure whom Manet had created in his painting of *The*

Baudelaire wearing a hat. *1867–68.*
Etching, first state, 10.9 × 9 cm
Bibliothèque Nationale, Paris

Absinthe Drinker (see page 7).

Baudelaire was more widely known as a critic and journalist than a poet. *The Painter of Modern Life*, probably written 1859–60, was first published in November 1863. In it he expands and elaborates previous ideas which he had put forcefully in his Salon reviews of the mid-1840s. Baudelaire was one of the strongest advocates of the attitude *il faut être de son temps*, and he was not alone in urging that artists and writers be of their time. Some thirty years previously writers had suggested that painters should depict contemporary life rather than the historical subjects favoured by the Academy. Baudelaire differed because he saw heroism in modern life: 'the life of our city is rich in poetic and marvellous subjects'. Why despise the fleeting, transitory moment? He urged painters to record the manners and customs of their own society in a sincere style and not to neglect the lower classes. 'Since all centuries and peoples have their own form of beauty, so inevitably we have ours' he wrote. Manet was profoundly influenced by his friend's enthusiasm for modern life and found fleeting images like *The Street Singer* worthy of recording in paint (page 61).

Baudelaire's hero was the painter Constantin Guys, and he admired his 'vigorous taste for reality, modern reality'. According to Baudelaire, Guys 'makes it his business to extract from fashion whatever element it may contain of poetry within history, to distil the eternal from the transitory'. These comments were to become even more applicable to Manet than to Guys. However, by 1863 Manet had tackled few contemporary subjects and although *The Absinthe Drinker* and *The Old Musician* made reference to current social issues, the clothes and situation of the figures designate them as specific types who do not belong to a particular age or place.

Manet decided to paint a scene from contemporary life; *Music in the Tuileries Gardens* is a direct response to Baudelaire's cry for a painter to 'snatch the epic quality from the life of today and make us see and understand with brush and pencil how great and poetic we are in our frock coats and patent leather boots'. The Tuileries gardens were, Théodore Duret informs us, 'a centre of sumptuous occasions . . . the concerts to be heard there twice a week attracted crowds of elegant society'. Manet and Baudelaire went to this fashionable meeting-place of the bourgeoisie in the afternoons to study the setting for the painting. In it, Manet gathered more than fifty people in an informal, animated crowd, representing his friends, the artists, poets, critics and musicians with whom he socialized during the early part of his career. Manet and Baudelaire themselves appear with

the painters Albert de Belleroy and Fantin-Latour, the critics Zacharie Astruc, Champfleury and Gautier and the composer Jacques Offenbach.

In 1863 Manet had an exhibition at the gallery owned by Louis Martinet on the boulevard des Italiens. He showed fourteen pictures including *The Street Singer*, *Lola de Valence* and *Music in the Tuileries Gardens*. The latter caused an outcry: it had no finish or detail, it was slapdash. Most of all, the Parisians hated seeing themselves in fashionable dress which would be out of date the following year. Such hostile criticism meant that Manet found no buyer for his paintings. He was fortunate, however, in that he came from a wealthy family and had inherited a substantial income when his father died in 1862. The following year was to be extremely eventful in both his private and public life.

Having just reached his thirties, it seems that Manet wanted to lead a respectable life and in October he married Suzanne Leenhoff. Manet met Suzanne in 1850 when, as an accomplished musician from Holland, she was employed to give piano lessons to his younger brothers. Presumably Manet's father did not approve of their liaison as they did not marry until after his death. Respectfully, the couple waited a full year in order to comply with the official mourning period of Manet's mother. It is fascinating that Manet should choose Suzanne for a companion. One friend unflatteringly commented that 'as a Dutchwoman she is the shape and size appropriate to her country', and, more charitably, 'besides this she seems fair and gentle'. She was calm and placid which was probably an ideal balance for Manet's excitable nature. She also had a child, Léon Leenhoff, who was born in 1852 and whose existence had been kept secret. Manet may or may not have been the natural father: Léon was always known as Suzanne's younger brother. Nonetheless, Manet treated him as a son. He often asked Léon to sit for his paintings (he can be seen in those reproduced on pages 47 and 93, for example) and, after Suzanne, Léon was the beneficiary of his will.

It was also in 1863 that Manet exhibited *Le déjeuner sur l'herbe* which secured his position as a revolutionary in the eyes of the public, and for many years ensured that he was unable to exhibit without causing a scandal.

By this time Manet had found himself a model with whom he could work. Victorine Meurent had been a model in Couture's studio and had a reputation for talking argumentatively while she posed. Manet had spotted her in a crowd and she had posed for him for several of his Spanish works, dressed in the costumes he collected. Her striking features are captured in *Le déjeuner sur l'herbe* and again in *Olympia*. It was partly the fact that Victorine's features are recognizable in these paintings which caused such an outcry. Manet did not paint her in the traditional way an artist used his model, where forms were idealized or made indistinct, but as a recognizable individual.

The Salon jury of 1863 were particularly severe. Count Nieuwerkerke, the Director-General of Museums, decided that year that only three entries per artist were allowed and that those who had already won first and second class medals could exhibit automatically, without having to present their paintings to the jury. This obviously meant that artists with no official awards were less likely to have their works accepted, and as Manet had only won an honourable mention, his chances of success were slim. For the public, the decisions of the jury were final. One year the jury was cruel enough to stamp an 'R' on the stretchers of rejected works which consequently meant that the paintings were unsaleable. (A buyer would return a painting which he had previously bought and expect to be refunded if his purchase was rejected by the jury.) The main responsibility for choosing the exhibits for the Salon in 1863 fell on reactionaries; Emile Signol, for example, who had won the Premier Grand Prix de Rome for History Painting in 1830, was a bigoted supporter of the academic tradition. Manet had submitted *Le déjeuner sur l'herbe*, *Mademoiselle Victorine in the Costume of*

an Espada and *Young Man in the Costume of a Majo*. All three were rejected. Some 3,000 artists had submitted about 5,000 works and only two fifths of these were accepted.

An outcry ensued, which came to the attention of Napoleon III, and the Emperor decided to go and see the rejected works before the official opening. He probably had little appreciation of art and was unable to see much difference between the rejected works and those which had been accepted, so he decided to have the former exhibited in a separate part of the building. This decision might have been prompted by the fact that panels commissioned by the Empress Eugénie for her salon in the Elysée Palace were amongst the rejected works, but the prime motive was his desire to be seen as a reformer, a liberal Emperor who would let the public reach their own conclusions.

Napoleon III's unprecedented idea for a Salon des Refusés set confusion amongst the potential exhibitors. Those who did not want to participate could inform the administration and their works were returned. But to withdraw would be admitting defeat.

These artists are in an awkward position. They are now free to exhibit. They can no longer complain that everyone is trying to stifle their immense talent. They have mocked us for too long with their insults and their ridiculous pretensions. They are now obliged to surrender themselves to the just mockery of the public. Those who withdraw are the feeble ones of the studios.

To exhibit, on the other hand, meant exposure to a hostile audience and many did in fact choose to withdraw. Manet welcomed the challenge of the Salon des Refusés and exhibited his three rejected paintings and also three etchings alongside canvases by Johan Barthold Jongkind, Camille Pissarro, J.A.M. Whistler and Fantin-Latour, among others.

Since 1855, the Salon had been held at the Palais de l'Industrie. Built for the World's Fair, the new venue

Fête Champêtre. *c.1510.*
Giorgione. Oil on canvas, 105 × 136.5 cm
Musée du Louvre, Paris

was intended to dissociate the works on show from the masterpieces at the Louvre, where the Salon had been held previously. The building was used for a variety of purposes from exhibitions of machinery to horse shows, and clearly did not provide ideal conditions for exhibiting works of art. Although the rooms for both the official and unofficial exhibitions were decorated in the same style, the exhibition of rejected works turned out to be a jumble. Without a jury the quality of works on show at the Salon des Refusés ranged from good to bad and the hanging administrator put up works as he found them, making no attempt to display them logically (for example, by separating landscapes from portraits). Some thought that the confused result was deliberately engineered in order to protect the jury of the official Salon, or else to embarrass the Emperor.

The public went to the Salon des Refusés expecting a scandal. In the first few hours about 7,000 visitors were received, more than at the official Salon. Man-

The Judgement of Paris.
*Marcantonio Raimondi after Raphael. Engraving
The Metropolitan Museum of Art, New York*

---

et's *Le déjeuner sur l'herbe* caused hysteria. What viewers saw was a nude in the company of two fashionably-dressed Parisian men. Manet had drawn on Giorgione's *Fête Champêtre*, which had been hung respectfully in the Renaissance rooms in the Louvre, and he had taken the composition directly from Marcantonio Raimondi's widely circulated engraving of Raphael's *The Judgement of Paris* (see page 15 and above). The public considered Giorgione's theme of two clothed gentlemen in the company of female nudes highly inappropriate for contemporary times.

Napoleon III, who had a string of mistresses, turned away in disgust, probably because he thought Manet intended to expose the loose morals of the Second Empire. Napoleon demonstrated his artistic preferences by purchasing Alexandre Cabanel's highly admired *The Birth of Venus* from the official Salon (see opposite). Paintings of sensuous female nudes proliferated at the Salon every year with such meaningless titles as Venus, Diana, Sappho, Psyche or the Daughter of Eve. Cabanel's nude inspired eulogies which now seem somewhat ridiculous. One enthusiastic critic wrote:

One cannot praise too highly the virgin purity of the neck, the simplicity of the stomach, the supplely undulating turn of her hip, the pallor of her thighs, the delicate formation of her feet right down to her bent toe, to her curled fingers, as they are often done by Correggio.

The Salon des Refusés caused an entirely different reaction:

On entering the present exhibition of refused pictures, every spectator is immediately compelled, whether he will or no, to abandon all hope of getting into that serious state of mind which is necessary to a fair comparison of works of art. That threshold once past, the gravest visitor bursts into peals of laughter.

Whistler's *White Girl* was the most prominent work in the exhibition, but Manet's *Le déjeuner sur l'herbe* provoked competition amongst the critics to see who could write the wittiest piece of derision. Zola later wrote in his novel *L'Oeuvre* an account of the sensation Manet caused:

The rumour that there was a funny picture to be seen must have spread rapidly, for people came stampeding from every other room in the exhibition and gangs of sightseers, afraid of missing something, came pushing their way in, shouting 'Where?' — 'Over there!' — 'Oh, I say! Did you ever?' And shafts of wit fell thicker here than anywhere else. The subject was the main target for witticisms. Nobody understood it; everyone thought it was 'Mad' and 'Killingly funny'. 'There, do you see, the lady's too hot, but the gentleman's wearing his jacket, afraid of catching a cold'. — 'No, that's not it! She's green, can't you see! Must have been in the water some time when he pulled her out. That's why he's holding his nose'. 'Pity he painted the man back to front, makes him look so rude somehow!'

The Birth of Venus. *c.1863.*
Alexandre Cabanel. Oil on canvas, 130 × 225 cm
Musée d'Orsay, Paris

It is not known if Manet had any idea of the scandal his painting would cause and, of course, there is the view that even adverse criticism has some value, especially when Manet's work was singled out for such attention from the vast number on display. We are reminded of Baudelaire's dandy who enjoys 'the pleasure of astounding people combined with the arrogant satisfaction of never being astounded oneself'. Manet was, however, never able to exhibit again without causing controversy.

The majority of Manet's critics thought that it was his technique that was unacceptable. His master Couture had hounded him because 'you refuse to see the succession of intermediate tones which lead from shadow to light'. What the critics were unable to see was that Manet transformed the way in which oil paint was applied, a transformation which subsequently had a profound influence on contemporary and future painters. Manet ignored the traditional method of building up a work with layers of paint and describing form through subtle modulations of colour. He abandoned the half tones and painted with a looser, more expressive brushwork. Manet would often prime his canvas with a pale colour and then apply the paint directly. This method led people to think erroneously that he worked at great speed. Antonin Proust records that when Manet was in the city he would make numerous sketches in his notebook of 'a nothing, a profile, a hat . . . the least object or detail of an object which caught his attention was immediately fixed on paper'. However, there is obviously a great difference between sketching in a notebook and painting in oil. Baudelaire thought that 'in trivial life, in the daily metamorphosis of external things, there is a rapidity of movement which calls for an equal speed of execution from the artist' and wanted the painter of modern life to attack his work with 'a fire, an intoxication of the pencil or the brush amounting almost to a frenzy'. Many of Manet's later paintings appear to have spontaneity, which was the effect he desired, but his results were achieved

through a slow and deliberate process. *Le Bon Bock* was said to have taken more than eighty sittings to complete (page 103).

The painter Charles Toché met Manet by chance in Venice in 1874 and witnessed him at work. He recalled a conversation with Vollard who had said 'any picture by Manet certainly suggests brushstrokes put down definitely, once and for all'. Troché replied

Wait a bit. That was what I thought before I had seen him at work. Then I discovered how he laboured on the contrary, to obtain what he wanted. The 'Poles of the Grand Canal' [The Grand Canal, Venice, page 115] itself was begun I know not how many times. The gondola and gondolier held him up an incredible time. 'It's the devil' he said, 'to suggest that a hat is stuck firmly on a head, or that a boat is built of planks cut and fitted according to geometrical laws'.

Zola informs us that 'in beginning a picture [Manet] could never say how the picture would come out'. Duret also wrote that the painter 'conducted himself with such boldness that you could say that there entered into his work a great degree of impulse and that he had no knowledge of a fixed method'. Manet's paintings would undergo considerable changes as he worked on them. He might scrape off paint to allow ground to show through or, if he was displeased with the effect, he would scrape away and repaint over and over again. 'At the moment all his admiration is concentrated on Mlle Gonzales, but the portrait makes no progress. He tells me he is at the fortieth sitting and the head has again been scraped off. He is the first to laugh about it' his colleague Berthe Morisot wrote in 1870.

As well as criticism for what was seen as a slapdash approach, Manet was accused of painting with colours which were too bright. *Music in the Tuileries Gardens* was seen as too harsh; 'the medley of red, blue, yellow and black, are the caricature of colour and not colour itself'. This is difficult to accept today

Venus of Urbino. *1538.*
Titian. Oil on wood, 117.5 × 162.5 cm
Galleria degli Uffizi, Florence

because of the subsequent movements in art which used vivid colour as the prime means of expression. Manet was not only a superb colourist but also, throughout his career, used black, white and the vast number of shades of grey in between as an important part of his work. This led to one of the most common criticisms, that his paintings were flat.

In 1865 the way in which Manet painted came under vigorous attack. Manet had painted *Olympia* in 1863, but did not present it to the Salon until 1865, perhaps because he hoped that the scandal of *Le déjeuner sur l'herbe* would have died down. Determined to be more lenient, the jury of that year accepted *Olympia* but as soon as it was exhibited it was considered outrageous and was subjected to an onslaught of hostile criticism (page 67). *Olympia* was described as 'a sort of female gorilla, a grotesque in India rubber outlined in black'. Manet had painted an interpretation of an old master theme as if to set his mark with the artists he emulated. Giorgione, Titian, Velázquez and Goya had all executed masterpieces of the reclining nude. It seems as though Manet was deliberately defying the Salon's admiration for Cabanel's *The Birth of Venus*. By modernizing Titian's *Venus of Urbino* (see page 19), Manet had presented, not an idealized nude floating dreamily across the water, but a frank confrontation with a successful prostitute.

Prostitution was extremely topical in mid-nineteenth-century France. In 1872 the writer, Paul de Saint-Victor wrote:

Courtesans exist in all times and places but has there ever been an epoch in which they made the noise and held the place they have usurped in the past few years? They figured in novels, appeared on stage, reigned in the Bois, at the races, at the theatre, everywhere crowds gathered.

The public preferred to ignore the truth and, if female nudes were to be represented in art, they wanted to see inviting, submissive figures. However, it was not the fact that Manet was dealing overtly with an embarrassing aspect of the Second Empire that upset the public so much as his technique. The composition of white on white and black on black showed no respect for the modelling of form or conventional perspective. Even Courbet said 'It's flat. There's no modelling. You could imagine she was the Queen of Spades on a playing card.'

Manet's unconventional treatment of pictorial space was influenced by Japanese prints which were becoming increasingly available. Japan had been in relative isolation until the invention of the steamship which made access quicker and easier. During the second half of the nineteenth century many aspects of Japanese culture became a European passion. Manet was one of the earliest customers of La Porte Chinoise, a shop which had opened in 1862 on the rue de Rivoli. It was run by M. and Madame Desoye who sold oriental wares of all kinds, including cheap prints. These prints may have arrived in France as wrapping paper for the china, lacquerware and other fragile objects imported; Monet even remembered

buying a piece of cheese wrapped in a Japanese print! 'Japonism' became highly fashionable; tea shops opened, drawing rooms were decorated with silks, fans and bamboo furniture, textile designs were copied, gardens recreated, and later, European music was set to Japanese stories; Gilbert and Sullivan's *The Mikado* appeared in 1885 and Puccini's *Madame Butterfly* in 1904.

The style and subject matter of the Japanese print offered an exciting alternative to the traditions of Western art and they have inspired European artists for decades. The surface of the print is divided into simple areas. An elegant black outline describes form with incredible economy of means. There are no shadows and the colours are printed in flat blocks. There are large empty spaces because of the tradition of executing Japanese paintings on silk; the beauty of the material did not require covering like the Western canvas. The Japanese painted on scrolls and their compositions, therefore, usually have a vertical format with high or low viewpoints placing the background and foreground into the same plane. Compositions can be asymmetrical and forms can be incomplete or cut off. This results not in discord but in a tranquil, static image with an overriding decorative quality. The subject matter often appears to be drawn from everyday life; women informally reading letters or playing musical instruments or taking tea in the garden, and many depict women at their toilet. Edgar Degas, Claude Monet, Pissarro, Whistler, Paul Gauguin and Henri de Toulouse-Lautrec were among those who in one way or another were influenced by the Japanese print, but Manet can be counted as one of the first to see their potential. Manet owned Japanese wares — a screen, silk hangings and china objects — which he used as props in the studio and they appear in several of his paintings. He was also influenced by certain aspects of the style of the Japanese print. This is most clearly evident in *The Fifer* (page 83) which was again described as looking like a playing card because of the lack of modelling and the startling economy with which Manet painted it.

Manet was also enthusiastic about developments in nineteenth-century print-making in France. An immense number of papers, magazines and periodicals as well as books was produced which meant that printed illustrations were in great demand; 13,000 illustrated publications were launched between 1830 and 1900. Traditionally, an artist would have his paintings reproduced as etchings, imitating his compositions exactly, in order to popularize his art by reaching a wider audience through a more accessible medium. Manet's knowledge of many of the works by old masters was obtained through these printed reproductions. Manet himself executed some 300 prints during his lifetime, most of which were after his own paintings, and he probably intended to publish them. However, Manet departed from tradition in that he etched his own works, not as an exact image of the original, but as a reinterpretation more suitable for a different medium.

Manet was also one of the first to take a serious interest in lithography. Etching requires the artist to cut his design into a wax surface deep enough to touch the zinc or copper plate which the wax covers. Acid then bites into the exposed parts of the plate forming the grooves which hold the ink for printing. Lithography offers a much easier method because it comes closer to drawing; a water-resistant crayon which will hold the ink is drawn onto stone. In spite of the alterations he made from the original, Manet's etchings are usually fairly close interpretations of his own oil paintings, another indication of his desire to maintain tradition. But Manet had a totally different attitude to the relatively new medium of lithography: with no traditions attached to it, he was able to create entirely independent compositions. It was not until after Manet's death that the print came into its own, as an independent art form, an achievement which Manet had done much to promote.

Manet was a founder member of the Société des Aquafortistes, established by the publisher Cardet in 1862 to encourage an interest in prints. Manet was sent three stones with instructions to draw on them whatever he wanted for an album with which Cardet intended to launch the Society. Manet portrayed a balloon ascent and used only one stone (see page 22). The printers were accustomed to impeccably finished designs and did not appreciate Manet's free handling;

Two courtesans, One Reading a Letter and the Other Playing the Samisen.
Kitigaro Utamaro. Late eighteenth-century woodblock colour print, 32.1 × 19.1 cm Victoria and Albert Museum, London

The Balloon. *1862.*
Lithograph, 39.5 × 51 cm
The New York Public Library

after just one proof they pursuaded Cardet to abandon the project. A balloon ascent was one of the most popular forms of entertainment in Paris and usually images of the scene were depicted as bird's-eye views. Manet's view is seen from the ground as if by one of the crowd in order to be able to give an enormous amount of information. *The Balloon* shows the many different types of people who took part in such events; a smart lady in a veil to the left, a worker in a smock with a child on his shoulders, a gentleman in a top hat, a seller with a jug pouring drink for two children and two bare-headed working-class women. We also see the booths where pantomimes were performed, banners, acrobats and the balloon itself, blown off-centre by the wind, like the flags above.

To illustrate how Manet felt the balloon represented the modern age, he placed one in full flight at the top right-hand corner of his painting of the *View of the*

World's Fair of 1867 (page 85). These international exhibitions were intended to demonstrate the progressive ideas of the Second Empire towards industry, commerce and art. This was the second of its kind held in Paris, the first having taken place in 1855. Manet's friend, Théophile Gautier, who is seen in *Music in the Tuileries Gardens* talking to Baudelaire, was one of the first to write on the poetry of industrial progress. He saw the locomotive as the modern Pegasus, he prophesied that the horse would become like the dinosaur and he saw how the use of machines could be a substitute for arduous labour. He was also enthusiastic about the balloon. He thought that once it could be directed on course, man would become master of the planet, national boundaries would disappear and there would be no more wars. Also famous for his balloon ascents, Gaspard-Felix Tournachon, known as Nadar, was one of the more colourful figures of the nineteenth century. He was a painter and caricaturist but he is most important for the remarkable photographs he took; he opened a studio at 35 boulevard des Capucines in order to encourage the process. He was extremely innovative and took photographs of contemporary life as well as aerial views of Paris from his balloon. He was also responsible for taking several photographic portraits of Manet and his contemporaries (see page 42).

Developments in photography were rapid in the mid-century. Some artists felt that it was a threat to their art; Paul Delaroche went so far as to claim 'From today painting is dead'. Others saw it as one of the most exciting scientific developments of the period and they realized how photographs could be exploited. Manet relied on them for several of his works. The etching of Baudelaire is taken from a photograph by Nadar as were some of the other likenesses in *Music in the Tuileries Gardens*. Manet used the photograph as he might a sketch, to see the features of a person not present. But the flat, black and white photograph also offered new ways of seeing. On the one hand it emphasized strong tonal contrasts of light and shade but, on the other, it

stimulated painters to realize the potential of colour and a greater freedom in the application of paint. It was these elements of painting that Manet developed.

Constant rejection by the Salon jury and ridicule from the press drove Manet to seek alternative ways of reaching the public. His *The Fifer* and *The Tragic Actor* were rejected by the Salon jury of 1866. The next year he decided not to submit again. Instead, following the example of Courbet, he had a wooden shed built in which he exhibited fifty-three of his paintings. This 'pavilion' was in the place de l'Alma, deliberately situated near the World's Fair, in order to attract as many visitors as possible. Baudelaire, Manet's closest journalist friend, was unable to give his support because in 1864, plagued by financial difficulties, he had moved to Brussels. Manet wrote to him in 1865 regarding *Olympia*: 'I wish you were here, my dear Baudelaire, abuses rain on me like hail. I wish I could have your sound judgement on my pictures because all this uproar is upsetting, and obviously someone must be wrong'. Baudelaire only returned to Paris when he was already paralysed with his last illness. Suzanne Manet had entertained the poet by playing Wagner on the piano during his final months. He died on 31 August 1867.

Encouragement came instead from Emile Zola who was one of the first to write extensively in Manet's favour. Zola's interest in painting was initiated by Paul Cézanne, his boyhood friend. Together they went to the Salon des Refusés and Cézanne introduced him to the artistic milieu of Paris. Zola had come to Paris in his twenties when he began his relentless criticism of the Establishment and opposition to injustice. In 1866 he became a reviewer for the newly founded daily paper, *L'Evénement*. His article 'Mon Salon' of that year began by criticizing the jury, and then turned into a thundering defence of Manet's rejected works, an unprecedented act, concluding:

Since nobody is saying it, I will say it myself: I will shout it from the rooftops. I am so sure that M. Manet will be accounted one of the masters of tomorrow that I think it would be a sound investment, if I were a wealthy man, to buy all his canvases . . . . M. Manet's place in the Louvre is marked out, like that of Courbet, like that of any artist of original and strong temperament.

Manet wrote to thank him, 'happy to be defended by a man of your talent'. Letters of protest flooded into *L'Evénement* and Zola's contract with the paper was cancelled. Nevertheless, he continued to support Manet.

For his exhibition in the place de l'Alma, Manet published a tiny catalogue at Zola's suggestion, with a reprint of Zola's article. Manet's introduction outlined his reasons for holding the exhibition.

This artist was advised to wait. Wait for what? Until there are no more juries? He preferred to settle the question with the public, in fact what he would like to do is become reconciled with the public, whom others have made into his supposed enemy. For time acts upon pictures with an irresistible buffer that smooths out all their original uncouthness . . . . M. Manet has always tried to recognize talent wherever it happened to be and does not claim either to overthrow traditional painting or to create a new style. He has simply tried to be himself and not someone else.

The exhibition did not receive the success Manet had hoped for and once more Zola came to his defence and published a long essay dedicated to the artist. In gratitude Manet offered to paint his portrait which resulted in the informal representation of the novelist at his desk (page 89).

The centre of Manet's social and cultural life was still the café. With the new building developments in Paris, numerous new cafés opened throughout the city, many with their own individual characters, and they played an important role in society for all classes. Before the advent of electricity, at dusk when the light became too poor for artists and writers to continue their work, they would gather with their friends in cafés. Courbet, for one, had made the Brasserie des Martyrs the headquarters of his school of Realism.

Manet, with Baudelaire and the writer Edmond Duranty, first patronized the fashionable Café Tortoni and the more literary Café de Bade on the boulevard des Italiens. Manet then favoured the Café Guerbois, at 11 Grande rue des Batignolles (later avenue de Clichy) which had a more modest setting and was less crowded and noisy. It can be seen in a rare depiction of these gatherings in Manet's *A Café Interior* (see opposite). Manet could be found here, surrounded by friends and admirers, after 5.30 p.m. on most evenings; Thursdays were set aside for regular meetings. The Café was on one of Paris's new boulevards, formed in 1863 and near to the quarter where many artists and writers lived or had their studios. The growth of the area was stimulated by the Gare Saint-Lazare, enlarged for the third time in the 1860s, which gave easy access to the sites on the Seine and to the Channel ports where the artists painted. The location of the Café became known as an alternative artistic centre to the Ecole des Beaux-Arts on the Left Bank, which further confirmed Manet's position in the eyes of the public as an anti-establishment painter.

The group which met at the Café Guerbois was comprised of journalists and writers, and also of the most important artists who were later known as the Impressionists. Manet had first become aware of Claude Monet in 1865 when the similarity of their names caused confusion. Manet asked, 'Who is this Monet whose name sounds just like mine and who is taking advantage of my notoriety?' They had become friends in spite of their different social backgrounds and artistic interests. Monet later recalled how

in 1869 . . . Manet invited me to join him every evening at a café in the Batignolles quarter, where he and his friends would gather and talk after leaving their ateliers. There I met Fantin-Latour, Cézanne, and Degas, who joined the group shortly after his return from Italy, and the art critic

Duranty, Emile Zola, who was then embarking on his literary career, as well as some others. I myself brought along Sisley, Bazille, and Renoir. Nothing could be more interesting, than these causeries *with their perpetual clash of opinions. They kept our wits sharpened, they encouraged us with stores of enthusiasm that for weeks and weeks kept us up, until the final shaping of the idea was accomplished. From them we emerged with a firmer will, with our thoughts clearer and more distinct.*

Manet was one of the oldest of the group and was seen as the intellectual leader. Duranty remembers him 'overflowing with vivacity, always bringing himself forward, but with gaiety, an enthusiasm, a hope, a desire to throw light on what was new, which made him very attractive'. This enthusiasm and support was obviously a great encouragement to these artists whose paintings had also met with little success. Renoir's memory of Manet is most endearing: 'You

A Café Interior (The Café Guerbois). *1869.*
Pen and black ink on paper, 29.5 × 39.5 cm
The Fogg Art Museum

are the happy warrior, with hatred for none, like some old Gaul, and I love you for that cheerfulness in the face of injustice'.

Manet's mother obviously did not approve of these daily gatherings at the Café. She wrote to Fantin-Latour asking him to dinner, 'since Edouard, thank goodness, has given up going to that dreadful café', and asked him to 'help us keep him away from that place which is so dangerous for someone of his lively, spontaneous temperament'. Obviously Fantin-Latour was not successful and indeed, Manet did sometimes have violent arguments even with friends. On one occasion, in 1870, Duranty had published an unflattering article on Manet who 'was hurt to the quick, and when he rejoined his circle of friends, he went straight up to the malicious author of the article and, mad with indignation, told him exactly what he thought of him and boxed his ears'. A duel followed in which Zola acted as Manet's second. Paul Alexis, a friend of both Cézanne and Zola and one of the group who frequented the Café, reported that

completely ignorant of the art of fencing, Manet and Duranty threw themselves upon each other with such savage bravery that, when the four astonished seconds had separated them, their two swords appeared to have been turned into a pair of corkscrews. That very evening they had become the best friends in the world again.

Of the café crowd, Manet was closest to Degas. They had met in 1861, perhaps through their mutual friend Bracquemond, but it seems that Manet first spoke to Degas when he admired him copying a painting in the Louvre. They were both from the same class, Degas's family being bankers with aristocratic origins. Sharing elegant manners, intelligence and wit they quickly became friends. They both admired the works of the old masters; as Degas expressed it, and Manet would agree, 'The Museums are there to teach the history of art and something more as well, for, if they stimulate in the weak a desire to imitate, they furnish the strong with the means of their emancipation'. But they too

had rows and returned paintings each had given the other. Manet never forgot that Degas was still painting history subjects when they first met while Degas boasted that he painted the race track before Manet. Degas also made acid remarks and said of Manet that 'he was the worst painter in the world, never making a brush-stroke without the Masters in mind'.

Manet always sought to maintain his independence but his position as the protagonist of the avant-garde was undeniably confirmed in the eyes of the public with Fantin-Latour's *A Studio in the Batignolles Quarter* of 1870 (see opposite). Manet is seen with his brush at an easel painting a portrait of Zacharie Astruc and surrounded by, from left to right, Otto Scholderer, Auguste Renoir, Emile Zola, Edmond Maitre, Frédéric Bazille and Claude Monet, as if he were instructing them. The painting also confirmed that the group which gathered at the Café Guerbois was indeed *la band à Manet*. Predictably, the painting caused derision and led one caricaturist to rename the painting *Jesus Painting among His Disciples or 'The Divine School of Manet' religious picture by Fantin-Latour* (see below). There is no denying that the painting does pay homage to Manet and demonstrates the great respect that he commanded. Renoir

---

Jesus Painting among his Disciples or 'The Divine School of Manet' religious picture by Fantin-Latour. *Caricature by Bertall.*

A Studio in the Batignolles Quarter. *1870.*
Henri Fantin-Latour. Oil on canvas, 204 × 273.5 cm
Musée d'Orsay, Paris

later said 'Manet was as important to us [Impressionists] as Cimabue was to the Italian Renaissance'.

It is interesting to speculate on the topics of conversation that took place at the Café. All would have agreed that classical subject matter had no place in contemporary life, but discussions over style and methods of painting would have brought forward many different views. Monet was becoming dedicated to work *en plein air* in front of the motif. He believed that this was the only way of working in order to reproduce accurately the effect of light falling on figures and objects in a landscape. Manet's *Le déjeuner sur l'herbe* inspired Monet to paint his own version of the theme (see page 28) and this in itself is an indication of the importance of Manet's work within his circle. Monet depicted his own class, the *petit bourgeois*, without an allegory or a disturbing nude, simply enjoying the countryside outside Paris.

Le déjeuner sur l'herbe. 1865–66.
Claude Monet. Oil on canvas sketch, 130 × 181 cm
Pushkin Museum, Moscow

In this case Monet was too ambitious, and began a massive canvas, measuring fifteen by twenty feet. He wanted to paint the canvas out of doors so that his painting could record the figures in the landscape as they were seen, but its enormous size was unmanageable and he had to abandon it in favour of a smaller one. In the late 1860s, Manet was uninterested in working *en plein air*. He would agree with Degas that 'a Picture must only be made from a study painted from nature. It is composed beforehand in your mind.

These studies you have amassed are useful simply as supports, as valuable bits of information'.

The subject of the depiction of shadows may have been discussed at the Café Guerbois. Monet had discovered while working *en plein air* that shadows were more naturalistically described without black and he eventually eliminated black from his palette. For Manet, black often forms the main structure of his composition. Even the choice of subject matter painted by the artists of the Café Guerbois differed. While Monet's interest in landscape grew, Degas and Manet remained figurative painters. Monet, Renoir and Pissarro painted various scenes of Parisian life and the surrounding countryside, still lifes, their girlfriends, wives and families; familiar subjects of their everyday world. Manet's range of subject matter was far broader; in the 1860s, as well as the subjects listed above, he treated political and current events and religious themes and he continued to reinterpret paintings by old masters.

Manet was quick to respond to an event which was part of the American Civil War, when in 1864 the Union ship the *Kearsage* sank the Confederate *Alabama* off the coast of France at Cherbourg (page 75). Again, in 1867, he started work quickly on *The Execution of the Emperor Maximilian* as soon as the event had taken place. This project occupied him for more than a year and resulted in four versions and a lithograph (page 87). Napoleon III had made Maximilian Emperor of Mexico but then withdrew the military support he needed to maintain the position; Maximilian was captured by the Republicans and was executed by a firing-squad. This event shook France deeply and accelerated the decline in Napoleon III's popularity. Like Zola and Duret, Manet was an ardent Republican. Even aged sixteen he had written to his father from Rio 'Try to save us a good republic for our return, I do fear that Louis Napoleon is not

The Third of May, 1808. 1814.
Francisco de Goya. Oil on canvas, 266 × 345 cm
Museo del Prado, Madrid

very republican at all'. Manet may have wished to blame Napoleon for the execution and, indeed, the four versions and the lithograph were taken by the authorities as political criticism and were banned from being exhibited.

During the late 1860s Manet showed a profound interest in the work of Francisco de Goya. Manet clearly felt politically emotional about the Maximilian affair, devoting much time and energy to his related project, but the event also provided him with the artistic licence to reinterpret Goya's *Third of May, 1808* (see page 29). During the summer of 1868, Manet was inspired by a scene of figures on a balcony which reminded him of another painting by Goya, *Two Majas on a Balcony*, now held in New York. Manet's painting of *The Balcony* (page 95) obviously relies heavily on Goya for the composition, but here, Manet has no other motive than to translate a potent image into his own haunting version of a contemporary scene.

The group at the Café was disbanded when, on 18 July 1870, France declared war on Prussia over a question of prestige and the throne of Spain. Bazille enlisted in a regiment of Zouaves, well-known for their dangerous missions, and died in November at the battle of Beaune-la-Rolande. Renoir also enlisted but survived. Zola was exempt from service as the only son of a widow. Degas enrolled in the infantry. Monet and Pissarro fled to London. Manet had sent his family to safety to the south of France and frequented political meetings in Paris with his brother Eugène and Degas. Manet enlisted in the artillery of the National Guard and became a staff officer, with Ernest Meissonier as his superior, and Bracquemond, Pierre Puvis de Chavannes, Charles-Emile Carolus-Durand and James Tissot as fellow soldiers.

The Prussians were superior in number, experience and equipment and overcame the French army in one humiliating defeat after another. As the Prussians advanced on Paris, food shortages and diseases took

Two Majas on a Balcony. *1800–12.*
Francisco de Goya. Oil on canvas, 194.8 × 125.7 cm
The Metropolitan Museum of Art, New York

hold. Manet wrote to his wife that people were eating cats, dogs and rats; only the lucky could find horse meat. Also, it was bitterly cold. On 5 January 1871 the Prussians began to bombard the city and food supplies gave out completely. On 28 January Paris surrendered and on 1 March German troops symbolically occupied Paris for forty-eight hours. Following their withdrawal, the exasperated population of Paris rose up against the new government, which retreated to Versailles, and the Commune was proclaimed in the capital. During the first days of May, troops of the Versailles government bombarded Paris and entered the city on 21 May. For a week the capital was drenched in blood. On 28 May resistance ceased. Manet had joined his family in the South but returned to Paris before the last street battles and recorded the conflicts in *The Barricade* (page 96).

Following the horrors of 1871, the Third Republic was formed and survived until 1940. The first two decades of its existence were highly prosperous, the national income doubled, industrial production tripled, the French Empire expanded and Paris was considered the capital of Europe. The prosperity and greater stability of the years after the Franco-Prussian War provided a more congenial climate in which to work. Manet and his contemporaries were extremely prolific during the 1870s but it was not until the beginning of the following decade that their work was given the credit it deserved.

When Monet was in London during the Franco-Prussian War he met the picture dealer Paul Durand-Ruel. This was an extremely fortunate encounter: during the 1870s Durand-Ruel was virtually the only art dealer to buy the works of Monet and his friends. Obviously, he was an important financial support because, except for Manet and Degas, all the Impressionists had serious financial problems. Durand-Ruel was also a great moral support, carrying out his belief that 'A true picture dealer should also be an enlightened patron, he should, if necessary, sacrifice his immediate interest to his artistic convictions and oppose, rather than support, the interest of speculators'.

Back in Paris in 1871, Durand-Ruel admired two of Manet's paintings which he saw in the studio of the painter Alfred Stevens. He immediately bought them and the very next day went round to Manet's studio where he bought all the canvases he could see. This amounted to twenty-three paintings which he bought for 35,000 francs. Durand-Ruel also agreed to buy those works which Manet had lent to various friends, if they could be retrieved. In 1872 Durand-Ruel organized an exhibition in London in which Manet had the largest representation with thirteen paintings on show.

Although Durand-Ruel bought paintings from the artists of the Batignolles quarter, his patronage alone was still nothing like enough to support them. Furthermore, due to an economic depression in 1873, Durand-Ruel was unable to buy any works that year. These painters continued to be unsuccessful at the Salon and desperately needed to find other ways of reaching potential customers. They decided to hold an exhibition of their works at Nadar's photographic studio and, after some deliberation, they called themselves La Société Anonyme des artistes, peintres, sculpteurs, graveurs etc. Their exhibition took place from 15 April to 15 May, 1874. 'Société Anonyme' roughly translates here as a 'limited company', and the name was specifically chosen because it had no association with any style. Thirty artists took part, most notably Monet, Renoir, Degas, Pissarro, Morisot, Alfred Sisley, Eugène Boudin and Cézanne. Their paintings were considerably diverse in style, and they neither wanted to, nor could, label themselves as a group. The irony is that the critic Louis Leroy, on seeing Monet's painting *Impression: sunrise*, labelled the entire group 'The Impressionists', a title which was meant to be derogatory and did not in any way reflect their ambitions.

Manet adamantly refused to take part in any of the seven exhibitions the Impressionists held in his lifetime. Degas hoped to the very last that Manet would join the group: '. . . there must be a *Salon of realists*. Manet does not understand that. I definitely think he is more vain than intelligent'. Manet had had some success with *Le Bon Bock* in the Salon of 1873 and maintained his principle that the official system was the preferable way of gaining recognition. He expressed this view in his famous cry 'The Salon is the real field of battle; these little arenas bore me so'. He always remained independent, as Proust recalled: 'Never did he say "I will be an Impressionist, a Naturalist, a Modernist" '. Manet knew the controversy his works caused and was unwilling to exhibit with a group of artists of little reputation and of greatly differing standards. Indeed, the exhibition caused an uproar; it was visited by some 3,500 people, and the Impressionists were considered to be completely mad. The critics had a field day:

They take a piece of canvas, colour and brush, daub a few patches of paint on it at random, and sign the whole thing with their name. It is a delusion of the same kind as if the inmates of Bedlam picked up stones from the wayside and imagined they had found diamonds.

Despite Manet's attempts to remain detached, he was still thought of as one of the Impressionists. They were incorrectly seen as a group with a single purpose, with Manet at its head. He was, however, a loyal friend and continued to support the group. In the spring of 1877 he wrote to the critic Albert Wolff to recommend the work of 'my friends Messers Monet, Sisley, Renoir and Mme Morisot .... Perhaps you do not yet like this kind of painting, but you will. In the meantime, it would be very kind of you to mention it in *Le Figaro*'. This was a bold step because Albert Wolff liked to think of himself as the wittiest man in Paris and his articles could make or break a reputation. He wrote that 'the Impression which the Impressionists achieve is that of a cat walking on the keyboard of a piano or of a monkey who might have got hold of a box of paints'. He also continued to humiliate Manet and even wrote him an insulting obituary.

Manet's letter to Albert Wolff points out the work of four of the Impressionists as being worthy of his attention, one of whom was Berthe Morisot. Morisot had studied painting, with her sister Edma, as one of the accomplishments suitable for a female of the upper class to which she belonged. In 1868 she was copying a painting by Rubens in the Louvre and was

introduced to Manet by Fantin-Latour. She became a constant visitor to his studio and to the Manet house on Thursday evenings along with his closest friends. Her features obviously fascinated Manet because he asked her to pose for several of his canvases. She thought Manet made her look 'strange rather than ugly' in *The Balcony* but surely one of the most captivating images in Manet's work is the portrait *Berthe Morisot with a bouquet of violets* (page 99). Manet wrote ' . . . the Mlles Morisot are charming. Too bad they're not men. All the same, women as they are, they could serve the cause of painting by each marrying an academician, and bringing discord into the camp of the enemy!' In 1874, however, she became Manet's sister-in-law when she married his brother, Eugène; their daughter, Julie, wrote an interesting diary, *Growing up with the Impressionists.*

In the 1860s the Morisot family took holidays on the Normandy coast where Berthe was able to paint landscapes without being too conspicuous as a woman at work. Jean-Baptiste-Camille Corot noticed her talent and dedication and became a regular visitor to the Morisot house; he gave Berthe advice and encouraged her interest in painting out of doors. Edma gave up painting on her marriage but envied her sister's life in Paris and that she was able to continue 'to chat with Degas while watching him draw, to philosophize with Puvis and to laugh with Manet'. Berthe Morisot considered painting a profession before and after she became a wife and mother. Her brother told how 'she would vanish for entire days among the cliffs, pursuing one motif after another according to the hour and the slant of the sun'.

Berthe Morisot was involved with Impressionism from its inception and, against Manet's advice, was one of the founder members who agreed to form the society in December 1873. She took an active part in artistic discussions at gatherings at her house (it would have been improper for her to join the other artists in the cafés) and she was present at meetings held to arrange the exhibitions. As well as landscapes she painted interior and domestic subjects, the limitations of the world of women of her class, drawn from her own experience. Her friends and contemporaries had elevated the everyday and ordinary objects and, therefore, provided a forum in which she could belong. Berthe Morisot took part in all the eight Impressionist exhibitions, except in 1879, following the birth of her daughter. Manet admired *The Harbour at Lorient* and she gave it to him as a present which he lent for the first Impressionist exhibition. Like Monet, Morisot's interest in painting out of doors encouraged Manet to do the same and to experiment with the lighter Impressionist palette.

Manet also respected Monet's work and helped him financially several times. On one occasion, in 1875, Manet attempted to come to his aid anonymously in order to encourage his work. He wrote to Duret

Yesterday I went to see Monet, I found him very upset and quite beside himself. He asked me if I would find someone who would take ten or twenty of his paintings of their own choice, at 100 francs each. Would you like to come in on a deal with me – say, at 500 francs each? Naturally, none of us, and he above all, will be aware that we are mixed up in the affair. . . . we must realize that we are making an excellent deal and are at the same time rendering a service to a man of talent.

Manet's friendship with Monet came closest in the summer of 1874. At the end of the exhibition at Nadar's, Monet had tremendous financial problems and was unable to pay the rent. Manet found him a house at Argenteuil, fifteen minutes from the Gare Saint-Lazare at a point where the Seine widens, providing an ideal boating centre. Manet's family had a house on the opposite bank at Gennevilliers and he decided to spend several weeks of the summer there. It was at Argenteuil that Monet convinced Manet that working *en plein air* had great value. Manet learned and adopted many of the discoveries Monet had made. He applied brighter colour and smaller strokes. Monet constructed a boat, which was large enough

for him to sleep in, from which he painted the river. Manet was not interested in painting the river or landscape, but always the figure. He painted Monet absorbed in his work in his floating studio, Monet's family informally in their garden or he posed models and friends in front of their gardens, the river and its shores (pages 109 and 113). Frequently Renoir would come and join them to paint side by side, and their series of canvases evoke the happy, intimate summer days that these friends spent together.

Manet was, however, a confirmed city-dweller and always preferred to be in Paris. In about 1876 Manet changed his early-evening venue to the Café de la Nouvelle-Athènes in the place Pigalle. This café distinguished itself by having a painting of a large dead rat on the ceiling. Under Napoleon III it had been the meeting-place of the opposition; for the intellectuals Duranty, Courbet, Jules Castagnary, Léon Gambetta, Alphonse Daudet, Nadar and others. The politicians among them had risen to power during the Third Republic and their place in the Café was taken by Manet and his friends. Vivid descriptions of meetings at the Café de la Nouvelle-Athènes were given by George Moore in his *Reminiscences of the Impressionists* of 1906. Moore had come to Paris to study painting and he had likened the Salon to a library of Latin verses composed by Eton and Harrow masters. He frequented the Café de la Nouvelle-Athènes and his portrait was painted three times by Manet (page 129). He describes the Café with its partitions rising above the seated figures, and the two tables in the right-hand corner which were reserved for Manet, Degas and their friends. Moore admired the frank passion of Manet's convictions and his decisive voice. 'He who would know something of my life must know something about the Academy of Fine Arts. Not the official stupidity you read of in the daily papers, but the real French Academy, the Café'.

It was only in the late 1870s that the café itself provided a subject for painting and Manet and Degas were among the first to realize that café life held a rich

Absinthe. *1876.*
Edgar Degas. Oil on canvas, 92 × 68 cm
Musée d'Orsay, Paris

source of imagery. Degas's *Absinthe* of 1876 depicts two miserable figures sitting in the Café de la Nouvelle-Athènes (see above). He asked friends from the Café to pose for him; the woman is the actress, Ellen Andrée and the man, Marcellin Desboutin. Desboutin was one of the Café de la Nouvelle-Athènes's most regular customers and had drawn the Impressionist group from the Café Guerbois because of his colourful personality; he was a painter, etcher and professional Bohemian, claiming to have aristocratic origins and to have lost a large fortune which forced him to sell the huge castle in Italy in which he had lived. He succeeded in having a play accepted by

the Théâtre Français and was brilliant in company when allowed to indulge in monologues. Degas reveals little of this in *Absinthe* and paints Desboutin uninterested in the woman who shares his table, in one of the most depressing images of city life. Manet, on the other hand, does not reflect anxiety or loneliness in his associated pictures but, with a mastery of bright colour, in *The Plum*, *At the Café* or *Le Journal Illustré* depicts anonymous city-dwellers as objective 'slices of life' with an incisive understanding of urban existence (pages 123, 124 and 127).

One of Manet's closest friends in the second half of the 1870s was Stéphane Mallarmé. The poet had come to Paris in 1873 and recalls that he saw Manet every day for ten years. Mallarmé wrote articles in Manet's defence and enlisted him on several occasions to illustrate his own poetry and his prose translation of Edgar Allan Poe's *The Raven*. The edition was published in May 1875 by the American, Richard Lesclide, in Paris and limited to 240 copies, signed by the authors. Mallarmé's prose faced the original English text and Manet's four, full-page lithographs, exceptionally large for the time, were inserted in between the pages of the text (see opposite). Manet also drew a head of a raven for the front cover and a raven in flight to be used as an ex-libris. A poster was printed to launch the book which announced that the lithographs were printed on laid or China paper and cost twenty-five francs; a further ten francs would purchase another set of the illustrations.

Manet's first study for the head of the raven exists on a sheet which also includes three drawings of a Pekinese dog and eleven copies of Japanese signatures. Manet also painted a dog belonging to Théodore Duret, a friend and Japanese enthusiast, which Duret had brought back from Japan in 1872. The style closely resembles Japanese brush drawings and to maintain this effect for the prints Manet used a revolutionary technique of brush lithography. The result gives, with great economy and sureness of hand, precise representations of the actual elements of the poem. The fourth and last plate shows the ominous shadow of the raven and that of the author silhouetted against the floor to illustrate the lines:

And the raven, never flitting, still is sitting – still is
*   sitting*
On the pallid bust of Pallas just above my chamber
*   door;*
And his eyes have all the seeming of a Demon's
*   that is dreaming*
And the lamp-light o'er him streaming throws his
*   shadow on the floor;*
And my soul from out that shadow that lies
*   floating on the floor*
Shall be lifted – nevermore!

The Raven met with little success. It reached England where the painter Dante Gabriel Rossetti owned a copy but he did not appreciate Manet's economy of expression. In 1881 he wrote to Jane Morris about 'a huge folio of lithographed sketches from the Raven by a French idiot called Manet, who certainly must be the greatest and most conceited ass who ever lived. A copy should be bought for every hyperchondriacal ward in lunatic asylums. To view it without a guffaw is impossible'.

'The Chair'. *1875.*
Lithograph illustration from The Raven.
The British Library

As well as making numerous male friends, Manet was also a great admirer of women. He had an immediate rapport with Mallarmé's great love, Méry Laurent, who was described as 'an indifferent actress, but a courtesan of genius'. Baudelaire said that Manet could be a recluse at times and behave like a sick cat but 'curiously enough, the presence of a woman, any woman, would set him right again'. By many accounts, Manet was extremely attractive and obviously many women enjoyed his company. There have been suggestions that he had affairs but there is no real evidence to support this. Giuseppe de Nittis, a painter who was in Manet's company often in the late 1870s, felt sure that in spite of appearances Manet remained faithful to Suzanne. De Nittis told an amusing story about Manet following a slim, pretty young woman in the street:

Suddenly his wife came up to him and said laughingly, 'There, I've caught you this time.' 'Well, that's funny,' said Manet, 'I thought it was you.' But the truth is that Mme Manet was a rather hefty, placid Dutchwoman who looked nothing like a skinny little Parisienne. She told the story herself, in her smiling good humoured way.

Letters from Manet to his wife during the siege of Paris in 1870 show that he was genuinely missing her and was greatly concerned for her well-being.

The house always seems so sad when I return all by myself in the evening and find nobody home. You are wrong to reproach yourself for not having stayed behind . . . I did very much want you to go, in spite of missing you so much; . . . I spent a long time looking for your photograph. I found the album at last on the drawing-room table and I was able to look from time to time at your dear face. . . . How I look forward to the moment when I can see you again! . . . Goodbye, my dear Suzanne, your portraits are hanging in every corner of the bedroom so I see you first and last thing. . . .

Berthe Morisot was slightly jealous when Manet turned his attention to Eva Gonzalès, the twenty-year-old daughter of a novelist, who became his only pupil. She had studied under the fashionable genre painter Charles Chaplin and met Manet in 1869. Having agreed to take her into his studio he immediately set about painting her at work. The composition must have been contrived: she wears a white muslin dress, hardly practical for working in oils; she sits at an awkward distance from her easel, touching up a flower piece which has already been set in an elaborate frame. The large canvas progressed slowly and the full length portrait has a formality unknown in Manet's paintings of Berthe Morisot or other close friends (see opposite). Eva Gonzalès's work was strongly influenced by that of Manet, but ironically hers was accepted at the Salon and admired by critics. Manet was generous enough to write 'Every day now the newspapers are filled with your praises. As someone, from whom you have asked advice from time to time, allow me too to rejoice with you in your success, a success which you have merited for a long time'.

Isabelle Lemonnier was, along with Méry Laurent, Manet's preferred model in later years. She was the daughter of an important jeweller and younger sister of Madame Georges Charpentier, wife of the publisher of naturalist writers like Zola and the Goncourt brothers, who had one of the most brilliant salons in Paris. The Charpentiers were the first grand bourgeois patrons to give support to Manet and the Impressionists. Georges Charpentier was the editor of the fashionable magazine *La Vie Moderne* and opened a gallery with the same name for the Impressionists' benefit off the boulevard des Italiens. In spring 1880 an exhibition there was devoted to the work of Manet. He showed ten oils and fifteen pastels, hung against sumptuous Japanese textiles. The exhibition drew large crowds and although comments which had been repeated for some twenty years were brought up

Eva Gonzalès. *1870.*
Oil on canvas, 191 × 133 cm
The National Gallery, London

Isabelle Diving. *1880.*
Watercolour, 20 × 12.3 cm
Musée du Louvre, Cabinet des Dessins, Paris

and his drawings have a freshness and spontaneity about them. Above all, they have humour, especially in the image of Isabelle in a bathing suit of the time, about to dive, seen from the back in a rather unflattering position.

During the last years of his career, Manet was fascinated by Parisians in cafés and it is typical that he should be one of the first to be inspired to paint the night life of Montmartre, which Toulouse-Lautrec made famous in the years after Manet died. Montmartre was the closest village to the capital. Situated on a hill it was only half an hour's walk from the centre of Paris. Since medieval times there were windmills on the hill to grind the grain from the rich valley below and bakers came from Paris for the flour. There were vineyards on the south-facing slopes and they supplied the establishments which appeared in the area. These prospered because, outside the old city walls, they were exempt from tax. Parisians would go up to Montmartre and have an evening drinking inexpensively. By the end of the eighteenth century there were cafés with dance halls and firework manufacturers who lit up the hill over Paris on summer nights. Also situated here were the quarries of the famous plaster of Paris, whose labourers frequented the drinking-halls. When the quarries fell into disuse they became hideouts for criminals who could disappear in the labyrinths of underground passages. During the Franco-Prussian war, balloons were launched from Montmartre to keep Paris in touch with the rest of France, which is how Manet's letters reached his wife. During the Commune the hill was a stronghold of those who refused to surrender to the Government and after 1871, Montmartre, as an area devoted to pleasure, became a symbol of everything most shocking to the bourgeoisie. Parisians, therefore, associated the area with low-life, with the working class in search of cheap entertainment and with the riff-raff of society.

yet again, one critic was wise enough to see 'that this Parisian, who has been so often laughed at, is a true painter, and that he has recorded his Paris with the spirit, talent and originality of a great artist'.

During the summer of 1880 Manet was on holiday at Bellevue in Normandy and he sent Isabelle a series of illustrated notes which he worked up from his imagination. His letters expressed his affection for her

Montmartre escaped the first developments of Paris by Baron Haussmann and kept its picturesque streets and old houses until the end of the century, even though it became part of Paris as the eighteenth *arrondissement* in 1860. Writers were among the first to be attracted to the area; the Goncourt brothers' *Germaine Lacerteux* of 1864 tells the story of a fallen maidservant who roams Montmartre haunting the dance halls. Zola threw a party in the Elysée Montmartre to celebrate the success of *L'Assommoir* in which he described Montmartre still 'looking as though it were part of the country-side, with green trees shading the cheap taverns'. Corot, Sisley and Pissarro depicted its rustic views and even Vincent Van Gogh's painting of the Moulin de la Galette in 1886 shows that Montmartre was still entirely rural. Most of the population of Montmartre was working

class and the inexpensive entertainment was enjoyed by young working girls, domestic servants, labourers and workers in minor trades. Artists were attracted to the area for its picturesque qualities, its honest energy and because studios and accommodation were cheap and the local prostitutes made ready models. Renoir, the son of a tailor, settled in Montmartre and stayed for forty years. His house was near the Moulin de la Galette, one of the three remaining windmills, which

A Café, Place du Théâtre Français. *c.1877–78.*
Pastel on canvas, 32.4 × 45.7 cm
The Burrell Collection, Glasgow Museums

had been converted into a café-restaurant and held dances every Sunday. Renoir records with great *joie de vivre* those who drank and danced there in his painting *Le Moulin de la Galette* of 1876.

The café-concert had been a popular form of entertainment since the 1830s, when singers and musicians first appeared outside cafés on the Champs-Elysées, then inside establishments on the principal boulevards. Both Toulouse-Lautrec and Degas liked to paint the stars, the singers and acrobats: Manet's last major canvas is of a serving-girl. *The Bar at the Folies-Bergère* evolved in the traditional way in which Manet always developed his important canvases. He made numerous sketches, at the Folies-Bergère itself as well as in the studio, before tackling the main composition. He posed a model in his studio behind a makeshift bar covered with bottles. Manet has given great attention to an unobvious subject, a barmaid, and has created a masterpiece from what could be an ordinary everyday experience. Like *Le déjeuner sur l'herbe* and *Olympia*, *The Bar at the Folies-Bergère* is arresting because it demands the presence of a spectator. The barmaid looks out without focussing, lost in reverie, oblivious to her glittering surroundings, in the most striking evocation of urban life.

Even at the end of his life Manet sought official recognition through a public commission. In 1879 he wrote to the Prefect of the Seine about a project he had devised for the decoration of the Municipal Council Chamber of the new Hotel de Ville of Paris. Manet wanted

To paint a series of pictures representing 'The Stomach of Paris' (if I may use the expression so popular today and which illustrates my idea very well) with the different corporations in their own surroundings – the public and commercial life of today, I would include the Paris markets, the Paris railways, Paris bridges, Paris tunnels, Paris race courses and public gardens. For the ceiling there would be a gallery, around which would be shown, in appropriate action, all the men alive today who have contributed in a civic capacity to the grandeur and richness of Paris.

The letter was unanswered.

In 1881 Manet's bad health forced him to take his doctor's advice and rest in the country, and he rented a house with a garden in Versailles. He was unable to work on large canvases and began to paint outside again. He adopted small strokes and applied bright colour to a series of small paintings of the house and garden. Their apparent spontaneity reveals none of his frustrations; he complained 'The country has charms only for those who are not obliged to stay here'. When bad weather prevented him from painting, he wrote to friends saying how bored he was away from Paris and decorated his letters with ink drawings or watercolours.

On his return to Paris, Manet saw his old friend, Antonin Proust, who had become Minister of Fine Arts in a cabinet formed by Gambetta. One of Proust's first acts was to acquire for the State a series of paintings by Courbet, the contents of whose studio were then being sold at auction. He also put Manet's name on the list of those to be decorated with the Legion of Honour. When the 1882 Salon closed, Manet was at last officially nominated Chevalier de la Légion d'honneur, and finally received the official recognition that he had yearned for, but he accepted it with regret. When the critic Chesneau congratulated him and also conveyed the best wishes of Count Nieuwerkerke, Manet replied 'When you write to Nieuwerkerke, you may tell him that I appreciate his kind thought . . . He could have made my fortune; and now it is too late to compensate for 20 years' lack of success . . . .'

Manet spent another summer close to Paris, at Rueil (page 139). Suffering from a disease that attacked the nervous system he was too ill to paint on a large scale. He worked on pastels and watercolours, and wrote charming letters begging his friends to come and visit

A Modern Olympia. *c.1873.*
Paul Cézanne. Oil on canvas, 46 × 55.5 cm
Musée d'Orsay, Paris

him. When he returned to Paris in the autumn, his friends began to be alarmed about his condition. Winter brought no improvement and early in 1883 he was confined to his bed. As a result of paralysis, gangrene threatened his left leg and in April he was operated on, but the amputation failed to save him. Manet died on 30 April 1883.

Manet had realized that the advent of the Museum had created a new environment for art and that it was there that masterpieces were venerated. There is a romantic myth that artists of the latter part of the nineteenth century failed to receive the recognition that they deserved during their lifetime. This is not true, for example, of Monet or Renoir. Manet's contemporaries were never short of admiration and even the reticent Degas admitted 'He was greater than

we thought'. The attention he attracted whenever he exhibited, although defamatory, shows that the critics knew that Manet was a force to contend with. However, Manet's principal aspiration was attained after he died. The prices of his paintings began to escalate after his death, a common occurrence today, and in under a year a large memorial exhibition was held, ironically at the Ecole des Beaux-Arts. Manet's brother, Eugène, and his wife Berthe Morisot took an active part in organizing the show and the catalogue had an introduction by Zola. The exhibition was followed by a sale of the contents of Manet's studio which comprised ninety-three paintings and numerous pastels, watercolours and drawings. The total of the sale was 115,000 francs, a sum which Renoir considered beyond all expectations.

Financial reward gives some indication of an artist's popularity, but this had not been Manet's concern. In 1889 Monet dedicated almost the whole of the year to organizing a public subscription to buy *Olympia* for the State from Manet's widow. Pissarro and Renoir made donations at a time when they were extremely hard up. *Olympia* still provoked consternation; Berthe Morisot recalled that in 1889 the Director of French National Museums became irate at the very mention of the painting, 'insisting that as long as he was there Manet would never enter the Louvre'. The State, however, accepted *Olympia* as part of the National Collection. Originally they hung her, not in the Louvre, but in the Musée du Luxembourg. In 1907 *Olympia* was transferred to the Louvre and was hung next to Ingres' *Grande Odalisque*, confirming Manet's place among the greatest painters of the nineteenth century. She was not destined for a domestic setting. *Olympia* now hangs as an icon of Modern Art in the Musée d'Orsay, where she continues to fascinate.

1832 ❧ 1883

THE PLATES

After the failure of *The Absinthe Drinker*, a painting of a Parisian down-and-out (see page 7), Manet resolved to present a subject which would appeal to the Salon jury. Spanish musicians and singers were highly popular because they evoked the romantic ideas that nineteenth-century France associated with that country. *The Spanish Singer* was accepted by the jury of 1861 and attracted such interest that the officials, who had originally hung it too high, were required to reposition it more advantageously. The painting found favour with the critics who admired the pleasing subject, the lively figure, vivid colour and the debt it owed to Spanish masters, so much so that 'Velázquez would have greeted him with a friendly wink, and Goya would have asked him for a light for his *papelito*'. Possibly through the intervention of Delacroix, it was awarded an honorable mention at the end of the Salon.

The composition for *The Spanish Singer* was invented in the studio. Manet's model wears clothes which are not entirely Spanish, and if he did play the guitar at all he must have been left-handed. In spite of its sentimental and picturesque qualities, the picture also attracted praise, as a piece of observation from real life, from a group of young artists whose admiration for Manet was to place him at the centre of avant-garde movements in Paris.

The Spanish Singer

Painted 1860
147.3 × 114.3cm
The Metropolitan Museum of Art, New York

The Spanish school of painting had a very strong influence on Manet's early work. Both Velázquez and Goya had painted children assuming the role of adults in a slightly self-conscious fashion. *Boy with a Sword* is a costume piece intended to attract those fashionable members of Parisian society who liked to dress up their children. It was painted in Manet's studio in the rue Guyot and the model was probably Léon Leenhoff, the son of his future wife; Léon appears in more of Manet's pictures than any other member of the family. Here, Léon is dressed as a page for royalty or aristocracy, awkwardly carrying the sword, innocent of its danger.

In spite of its charm, Zola realized that this painting had

nothing to offend the weak eyesight of the many. Edouard Manet is said to have some kinship with the Spanish masters, and he has never shown it so much as in The Boy with a Sword *... If the artist had always painted heads like this, he would have been the darling of the public, showered with money and praises; true, he would have remained a mere echo [of the past], and we would never have known the sincere and harsh simplicity that is his great gift ....*

Boy with a Sword

Painted 1861
131.1 × 93.3cm
The Metropolitan Museum of Art, New York

The idea of painting a female nude has great significance in any artist's career – many masters have depicted the subject since the Renaissance (see page 19). Traditionalists and realists alike valued the theme and every Salon contained numerous examples. Baudelaire declared that the nude, 'the darling of the artists, that necessary element of success – is just as frequent and necessary today as it was in the life of the ancients'. In Courbet's monumental painting *The Studio* his nude model stands beside him as an attribute of the artist.

Manet worked on a series of small drawings, oils and prints of nudes in a landscape as studies for this canvas. They rely on copies Manet had made from old masters in the 1850s and serve to illustrate how he revered the work of his predecessors. Suzanne, Manet's future wife, apparently sat for this figure whose pose and attitude is reminiscent of those in works by Rembrandt and Boucher. Originally, Manet worked on a biblical theme, *The Finding of Moses* (which he never finished), from which he cut out this figure and retitled it. In 1861 it was sent to St. Petersburg as *The Nymph and Satyr*, and X-ray photographs show the face of a satyr in the upper right-hand corner of the canvas. It was only after this that Manet decided to remove all traditional anecdotal associations from the painting, to rid it of biblical or mythological narrative, and, except for the title, present the figure as a simple bather.

The Surprised Nymph

Painted 1859–61
144.5 × 112.5cm
Museo Nacional de Bellas Artes, Buenos Aires

This is the largest of Manet's early paintings, and it depicts a haunting group of figures, orphans and street urchins, an itinerant musician and an alcoholic, who were the people exposed by Baron Haussmann's new development of Paris, and were an embarrassment to the Second Empire. The boy wearing a ragged Pierrot-like costume may refer to the Théâtre des Funambule, the Parisian home of the *commedia dell'arte*, which was about to be demolished as part of the new city planning.

Manet's painting closely relates to Velázquez's *The Drinkers* for its composition, colouring and handling of paint, which broadly describes the forms with few shadows. However, individual figures were taken from a diversity of sources; the little boy in white is Watteau's *Gilles*, the cloaked figure with a hat to the right is a repeat of Manet's own *The Absinthe Drinker* of 1858–59 (see page 7), and while the musician is taken from Velázquez's painting of *The Drinkers*, he is also derived from a sculpted classical head in the Louvre. The Second Empire was fascinated by gypsies; there were many books and articles on their customs, paintings of them in the Salon, plays, ballets and operas about them. The supposed gypsy practice of stealing babies appeared in most literature and might explain why the child on the left of the picture is holding one. The figure on the far right may be a reference to a popular image of the 'Wandering Jew', a man isolated from society. The absinthe drinker holds Baudelairian associations of the philosopher who gets drunk on his own words. Manet might have known of Spanish images where philosophers were shown as beggars.

The loose composition and the ambiguous relationship between the figures was found disturbing by contemporaries. Although some of the figures look at others, none are in communication. The title suggests that the old musician has brought about this gathering but the painting is unexplained. This was Manet's last attempt to paint the lower classes in a semi-romantic, semi-realistic manner.

The Old Musician

Painted 1861–62
187.4 × 248.3cm
National Gallery of Art, Washington DC

The woman reclining on a sofa in Manet's newly-rented studio on the rue Guyot is Jeanne Duval, the mistress of his great friend Charles Baudelaire. Her identity as the sitter was confirmed by Manet's wife when an inventory was taken of the contents of the artist's studio after his death.

Baudelaire had once passionately loved this woman, calling her a 'Black Venus', and she had inspired many of his beautiful poems. She was born in San Domingo and was tall and angular with a dark complexion. She was twenty-one in 1842 when she first met Baudelaire and her features strongly appealed to his exotic tastes. Their relationship was stormy; Baudelaire would write that she was 'my one diversion, my one pleasure, my one companion' but also that she 'considers me nothing more than a servant, a piece of property ... [one] who would throw my manuscripts in the fire if that would bring in more money than letting them be published ... '.

When this painting was executed, Jeanne Duval was about forty-two and very ill. She had been an invalid, half paralysed, for almost fifteen years. Since 1859 she had been cared for in a sanitorium which Baudelaire managed to fund in spite of his lack of money. The large area dedicated to her dress was probably intended to disguise the awkwardness of her legs. Manet avoided giving much detail to her face which was racked with pain. Manet was generous to his friends and often gave them paintings but, given that this remained in his possession until his death, we may assume that Baudelaire was unhappy with the result.

Baudelaire's Mistress, Reclining

Painted 1862
90 × 113cm
Budapest Museum of Fine Arts

Manet's painting of a woman reclining on a couch alludes to Goya's two paintings, *The Clothed Maja* and *The Nude Maja*. It has been suggested that Manet's *Olympia*, painted the following year, and the picture shown here were intended to echo Goya's pair. However, although both paintings depict the reclining figure and both have cats in the composition, they are of different sizes and depict different models.

The rather stocky woman who posed for this work is thought to have been the mistress of Nadar, Manet's photographer and balloonist friend, who also felt a strong admiration for the work of Goya. Here, Manet has dressed his model in one of the Spanish costumes which, according to Zola, he kept because he liked their colours. He acquired them from a Spanish tailor on the rue Saint-Marc whose address is recorded in a notebook that Manet used between 1860 and 1862. Masculine disguise for women was popular during the Second Empire as contemporary literature records. Manet highlights the cream-velvet knee breeches and pale stockings more than the model's face, a highly provocative act for, in the days of the crinoline, male breeches were considered particularly revealing.

Young Woman Reclining in Spanish Costume

Painted 1862
94 × 113cm
Yale University Art Gallery, New Haven, Connecticut

anet first painted his most famous model, Victorine Meurent, who appears again in *Le déjeuner sur l'herbe* and as *Olympia*, in 1862. He spotted her when she was eighteen, in a crowd outside the Palais de Justice, and wrote down her address in his notebook. She had been a model in Couture's studio. She was known to be talkative and argumentative, and she became a painter herself, enjoying some success at the Salon.

Manet did not visit Spain until 1865 and *Mademoiselle Victorine in the costume of an Espada*, is, therefore, an invention. He posed Victorine in a costume from the collection in his studio, and in a pair of shoes which do not look suitable for bullfighting. The scene of the bullfight in the background is taken from one of Goya's *Tauromaquia* etchings. The painting was exhibited at the Salon des Refusés of 1863 and Manet was criticized for his lack of traditional perspective. It was probably his knowledge of Japanese prints which influenced the unconventional treatment of the pictorial space here.

It is interesting to note that an X-ray of the painting shows that Victorine originally held the cape in both hands and that the sword was added later. Manet also painted her over an entirely different figure, a seated female nude which does not relate to any other known work, having first turned the canvas upside-down.

Mademoiselle Victorine in the costume of an Espada

Painted 1862
165.1 × 127.6cm
The Metropolitan Museum of Art, New York

Lola Melea, known as Lola de Valence, was the star of Mariano Camprubi's Spanish ballet. During the Second Empire Spanish entertainment was highly popular and companies of dancers and musicians performed in the theatres of Paris. Lola was well known to Manet and his friends and was described by Baudelaire as a 'beauty at once darkling and lively in character'. Manet's depiction is presumably a frank one as he does not flatter her stocky figure and strongly muscled legs which are noticeable in spite of her distinctive features and brightly-coloured dress.

Manet was continuing a tradition of representing Spanish dancers on the stage. He invited Lola to come and pose for him in his studio with her feet in the fourth position used in classical dance. The painting is also reminiscent of Goya's full-length female portraits, the most famous of which is the *Duchess of Alba*. Originally the background here was plain, but Manet has added a view through the stage to the audience, as if Lola is about to perform.

Lola de Valence

Painted 1862
123 × 92cm
Musée d'Orsay, Paris

Antonin Proust recalled how once he was walking with Manet up one of Baron Haussmann's new Parisian boulevards to the artist's studio, when Manet immediately recognized a valid subject for a painting. 'Where the rue Guyot begins, a woman was coming out of a sleazy café, picking up her skirts, holding a guitar. Manet went up to her and asked her to come and pose for him.' She evidently refused as the model here is Victorine Meurent.

This was one of fourteen paintings exhibited at Louis Martinet's gallery in March, 1863. It was badly received because the image did not conveniently fall into a recognizable type. Most street singers of the Second Empire were unemployed and impoverished, going from bar to bar for very little reward and, if they were considered a subject worth painting at all, they were treated with anecdote and sentiment. Manet's street singer is not poorly dressed and is devoid of expression and emotion.

Manet was also criticized for his technique, which was considered crude. The picture is painted with economy and directness, with simplifications and few half-tones, which suggests that Manet has drawn on the stylistic traits of the Japanese print. The year this was painted Madame Desoye opened a shop where Japanese prints were sold and Manet was one of its earliest customers. Four years later Emile Zola was the first to write positively about this painting.

The canvas I like best . . . is The Street Singer *. . . it seemed to me that it analyses life with extreme simplicity and exactitude. A picture like this, over and above the subject matter, is enhanced by its very austerity; one feels the keen search for truth, the conscientious effort of a man who would, above all, tell frankly what he sees.*

Zola appreciated Manet's ability to succinctly capture an urban figure, in a world of her own, oblivious to people and place, an image which Manet tackled again at the end of his life with *The Bar at the Folies-Bergère.*

The Street Singer

Painted c.1862
171.3 × 105.8cm
Museum of Fine Arts, Boston

Manet has painted the fashionable society of the Second Empire, under the trees in the Tuileries Gardens, with men standing and women sitting on newly-designed wrought iron chairs. If there is a band, it is not in the picture and no-one seems to be paying any attention to it; all interest lies in making what is presumably polite conversation.

Many of the people depicted are likenesses of Manet's friends and serve as a catalogue of the people whose company he enjoyed. Manet appears himself on the far left with the painter Albert de Balleroy, with whom he had shared a studio; to the right of the centre, standing bowing in profile, is Manet's brother, Eugène; of the two ladies in bonnets sitting in the foreground the one on the left is Madame Lejosne, at whose house Manet met Baudelaire and Bazille. Behind these two, near the trunk of a tree, stands a group of three men. They are Charles Baudelaire in conversation with Théophile Gautier, an important literary figure, and Baron Taylor, Inspector of Museums and a passionate exponent of Spanish art in France. Although their features are vague, other figures in the composition have been identified. Manet intended this painting to be a gathering of his intellectual and influential friends in familiar surroundings, and inspired by Baudelaire's advocacy of the heroism of modern life painted a straightforward view of a contemporary scene.

In 1863 *Music in the Tuileries Gardens* was exhibited at Martinet's Gallery. The public thought it was outrageous and it incited such anger that one man attacked it with his umbrella. The painting was considered to treat a subject which belonged to magazine illustration. It was criticized for the lack of a focal point to the composition; it had no centre of attention, the colours were too violent and the technique so loose that it appeared to be merely a sketch.

Music in the Tuileries Gardens

Painted 1862
76.2 × 118.1cm
The National Gallery, London

anet's *Le déjeuner sur l'herbe* was a *succès de scandale* of the Salon des Refusés of 1863. Manet probably intended the painting to be a landmark in his career but the hysteria that it caused was unforeseen. The painting was taken as a social comment on the loose morals of the Second Empire and the ridicule that followed was probably a disguise for the embarrassment it caused. One outraged critic declared: '... I seek in vain for the meaning of this uncouth riddle'. This riddle remains unsolved today.

The composition evolved in a traditional manner. Manet made sketches out of doors on the Île de Saint-Ouen for the setting, and executed a substantial sketch in oil which is now in the Courtauld Galleries, in London. His favourite model at the time, Victorine Meurent, posed for the nude in the foreground and he recruited members of his family for the men; they are either his two brothers, Eugène and Gustave, or else the bearded figure is the young sculptor and Manet's brother-in-law, Ferdinand Leenhoff.

Antonin Proust recalled that Manet was inspired to paint this scene when they were watching bathers at Argenteuil. He was reminded of Giorgione's *Fête Champêtre* in the Louvre (see page 15), although the differences between his painting and that of the Venetian Renaissance master are subtle but vast. Giorgione's rustic arcadia shows two men absorbed in their music, unaware of the presence of the nudes. In Manet's painting the men seem indifferent to their female company and the nude turns to the spectator with a challenging stare.

The group of figures was taken directly from Marcantonio Raimondi's engraving of Raphael's *The Judgement of Paris*, depicting the mythological narrative in which Paris has to decide who is the most beautiful of the three goddesses, Venus, Juno or Minerva. In the foreground, Manet has introduced a basket of spilt fruit, a traditional symbol of lust and decadence, reinforcing the suggestion that the painting is an allegory that might indeed refer to the loose morals of the modern age.

Le déjeuner sur l'herbe

Painted 1863
208 × 264.5cm
Musée d'Orsay, Paris

The theme of the reclining nude was extremely popular in the Salon and has a long tradition in the history of art. Manet took the composition for *Olympia* from Titian's *Venus of Urbino* which he had copied in Florence (see page 19), but he also borrowed the figure's more challenging attitude from Goya. With this painting Manet intended to compete with these two masters and others, most notably Giorgione, Velázquez and Ingres. It was *Olympia*, albeit after his death, that secured Manet's place among the great masters in the museums.

The public were used to seeing pictures of nudes, sensually reclining for men to feast their eyes upon. Visitors to the 1865 Salon would have been in no doubt that in *Olympia* (a pseudonym for a Parisian *horizontale*) they were confronting a prostitute. Victorine Meurent posed for the figure because Manet found her features a perfect expression of modernity. She was described as the 'free daughter of Bohemia, artist's model, butterfly of the brasseries . . . with her cruel childlike face and eyes of mystery'. Paris had developed a subculture of eastern exoticism, and the black servant bringing in flowers evokes the pleasures of the harem. This expression of sexual freedom was entirely against the ethics of the Second Empire, which idealized the family while at the same time condoning a system of brothels for bourgeois husbands. However, Manet takes no moral stand.

This is not an image of a woman, worn out by hard labour, who has to supplement her low income in order to exist. Her surroundings indicate that she is successful at her profession and she is entirely in control of her situation. For Titian's innocent dog Manet substituted a black cat, which, with its arched back and bristling tail, acknowledges an intruder to *Olympia*'s domain. The image is uncomfortable because the woman is provocative but there are no signs which satisfyingly condemn her trade. Manet has painted *Olympia* as a person, not an object, and we are left with the sensation that if her charms were wanted, she would dictate the rules.

Olympia

Painted 1863
130.5 × 190cm
Musée d'Orsay, Paris

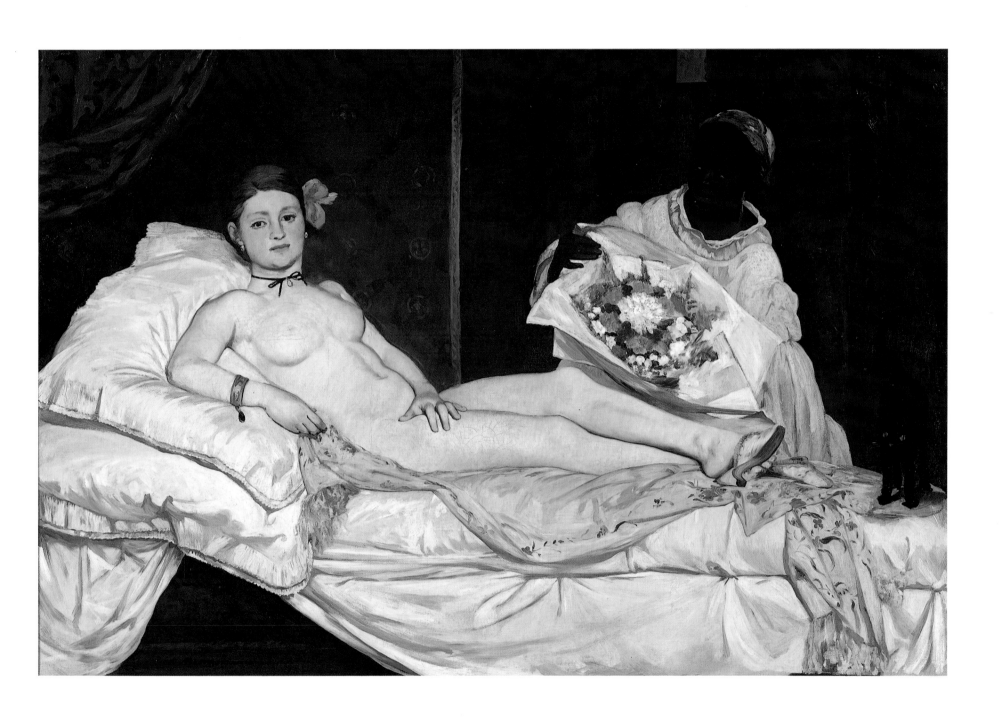

In 1864 Manet submitted to the Salon two paintings on the theme of death, *Episode from a Bullfight* and *The Dead Christ with Angels*. Both were accepted and predictably received adverse criticism from the public. *The Dead Toreador* was originally part of the large composition *Episode from a Bullfight*, which Manet cut up at some time between the Salon and his one man show of 1867. He may have been upset by criticisms of the relationship between the dead toreador in the foreground and the scene in the background, which was probably not dissimilar to the treatment of space in his *Mademoiselle Victorine in the Costume of an Espada* (page 56). However, the isolated figure is highly dramatic and Manet may have thought that the background was a distraction.

Both Salon paintings of this year draw on works by old masters and depict subjects Manet had never seen. This figure is derived from *The Dead Soldier*, thought to be by Velázquez, which was originally in the Pourtales collection in Paris and is now in the National Gallery in London. If Manet did not see the painting itself he could have known it from a photograph which was published by Goupil in 1863.

The Dead Toreador is a masterful composition in black and white and critics immediately realized Manet's debt to Spanish masters, dubbing him 'don Manet y Courbetos y Zurbaran de las Batignolas'. Baudelaire immediately came to his defence, recognizing the strength of a work which confronts death with an attitude that is indifferent, detached and devoid of all human emotion.

The Dead Toreador

Painted 1864
75.9 × 153.3cm
National Gallery of Art, Washington DC

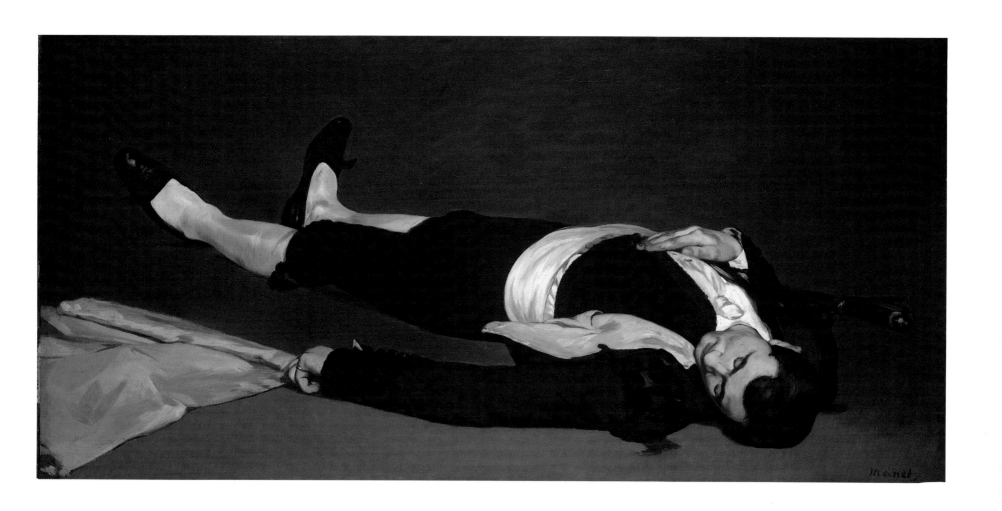

For the Salon of 1864 Manet presented a subject which had been treated by many old masters, especially by those of the Italian Renaissance. Baudelaire knew that Manet's work caused derision and sent a note warning him:

. . . it seems certain that the lance wound was made on the right side. Therefore it will be necessary for you to make a change in the position, before the opening [of the Salon]. Verify it in the four Gospels. And take care not to give malicious people cause to laugh.

The painting was accepted by the jury but again it was slated by the critics who thought that Christ's body looked like an unwashed corpse. The angels were described as 'two damp squibs that failed to go off'. Most of all, Manet was criticized for a lack of spirituality and for being incapable of creating the illusion of form through modelling.

Manet usually chose to paint the world in which he was familiar, models or friends posing in his studio, or slices of Parisian life. With this traditional old master theme he may have been responding to the challenge of Courbet who claimed that

Painting is an essentially concrete *art and can only consist of the representation of* real *and* existing *things. It is a completely physical language, the words of which consist of all visible objects; an object which is* abstract, *not visible, non-existent, is not within the realm of painting.*

Apparently Courbet teased Manet about painting angels – 'You've seen angels, to know if they have a behind?'

The Dead Christ with Angels
Painted 1864
179.4 × 149.9cm
The Metropolitan Museum of Art, New York

During Manet's career there were two periods in which he painted flowers. This canvas is one of a series of peonies he worked on in the mid-1860s, and he returned to painting smaller versions of flower themes, some eighteen years later, at the end of his life when he was very ill.

Still lifes of flowers, especially in Dutch art, may be seen as allegories of vanity, expressed by painting the transience of beauty. Manet's bunch of peonies includes a bud on the right, flowers in bloom and one which is already fading and has dropped some petals. However, Manet probably simply wanted to paint flowers he liked. His ability to depict them was the only part of *Olympia* which had received acclaim (page 67). Peonies had been introduced recently into Europe and during the Second Empire were considered a fashionable luxury. Manet grew peonies in his garden at Gennevilliers and the freedom of his brushwork is in perfect accord with the fullness of their blooms. As George Moore said, 'A piece of still life by Manet is the most wonderful thing in the world; vividness of colour, breadth, simplicity, and directness of touch – marvellous'.

Vase of Peonies

Painted 1864
93.2 × 70.2cm
Musée d'Orsay, Paris

This was the first painting Manet executed of a theme drawn from a current event: an incident from the American Civil War which occurred just off the coast of France and consequently received a great deal of attention. On 19 June 1864, the Confederate ship, the *Alabama*, was attacked and sunk near Cherbourg by the Union's ship, the *Kearsage*. The *Alabama* had been built in Liverpool and was disguised as a merchant vessel. Her commander, the flamboyant Raphael Seemes, took her straight to the Azores to be stocked with weapons and coal. She sailed for twenty-two months with the Confederate flag hoisted. Seemes claimed to have sunk sixty-five Northern ships and was a popular figure in both England and France.

After nearly two years at sea the *Alabama* was in need of repair. Seemes asked for permission to dock at Cherbourg and at the same time the Union ship the *Kearsage* pulled into the same harbour. The battle which sank the *Alabama* occured seven miles out to sea and was watched by thousands of Frenchmen. Manet had not been present but drew on the numerous reports which appeared in the newspapers.

Manet had spent nearly a year at sea in his youth and must have been excited by the chance to paint a topical subject which might appeal to a wide audience. Moreover, seascapes following seventeenth-century Dutch examples were traditional and highly popular. Manet was a Republican and would have supported the Southern cause, but he painted the event with objectivity and accuracy. In the foreground a French boat sails to save the men in the water; the little steamer on the right is the English rescue ship which took the Southerners to England, and the battle takes place on the horizon in the distance. Manet created an unusual composition, drawn from his experience at sea, and the perspective was much criticized. Water takes up about three-quarters of the canvas as if we are witnessing the scene from on board ship rather than from the shore.

The Battle of the *Kearsage* and the *Alabama*

Painted 1864
145 × 130cm
John C. Johnson Collection, Philadelphia Museum of Art

The race-tracks at Longchamp in the Bois de Boulogne were close to the capital and provided a popular day out for Parisian society. They formed part of the development of the new Paris during the Second Empire and were completed in 1857. Degas, his artistic rival, claimed that he had been the first to take the race-track as a subject of interest and he made numerous paintings, pastels and drawings of horses and jockeys between 1860 and 1900. Degas's studies, however, very rarely depict a particular race-track, or horse or rider. Manet's painting, on the other hand, is definitely Longchamp, the building seen on the right is the roof of the Tribune Publique and we look south down the track to the hills of Saint-Cloud.

The majority of Manet's works focus on figures and he may have been attracted to the fashionable spectators as subjects. Usually his paintings are static, but here Manet has chosen to depict the climax of a race. *Races at Longchamp* is an extremely daring and imaginative composition. Manet has placed us in an unlikely position at the middle of the track, with the horses thundering towards us. Traditional paintings and sporting prints of horse-racing, the most famous of which is Géricault's *Racecourse at Epsom* of 1827, show the horses from the side. Before the advent of photography which freezes movement, galloping horses were represented as if flying, with all four legs stretched out in mid-air. Manet's rendition, with the forms indistinct and incomplete as the horses kick up the dust, is a far more realistic description of a race.

Races at Longchamp

Painted c.1864
43.9 × 85.5cm
The Art Institute of Chicago

In March 1866, Manet told Baudelaire 'I have sent two paintings to exhibition ... A portrait of Rouvière in the role of Hamlet, which I am calling the Tragic Actor to avoid the criticism of those who might not find it a good likeness – and a fifer of the Light Infantry Guard ...'. Both were refused by the jury, that year a cry for another Salon des Refusés was denied, and Manet showed the pictures in his studio, but only to his friends.

The actor and painter Philibert Rouvière had created a name for himself at the Théâtre de Saint-Germain where he had played the dramatic role of Hamlet since 1846. He was admired by many including Baudelaire, Gautier and Champfleury. Rouvière's last performance was in 1865, when poor health prevented him from continuing. Friends rallied round, writing articles, organizing performances and holding a sale of his paintings on his behalf. Manet may have intended this painting as a gesture of support but Rouvière was already seriously ill and the portrait was unfinished when he died in October 1865.

A long tradition in popular French imagery placed actors in their famous roles in an undefined setting. Manet's portrait is also indebted to the work of Velázquez. From Spain, Manet wrote to Fantin-Latour:

The most astonishing example in [Velázquez's] splendid œuvre, and perhaps the most astonishing piece of painting ever done, is the painting listed in the catalogue as Portrait of a Famous Actor in the Time of Philip IV. *The background vanishes, and atmosphere envelops the good man, a vital presence dressed in black.*

Manet could be describing his own work.

The Tragic Actor

Painted 1865–66
187.2 × 108.1cm
National Gallery of Art, Washington DC

After the scandal of *Olympia* Manet went to Spain for the first time in 1865. The obvious delight he had in seeing paintings by Velázquez and Goya is recorded in letters he wrote to Fantin-Latour. He was also excited by the bullfight, and he wrote to Baudelaire that it was 'one of the finest, strangest, and most fearful spectacles to be seen . . . I hope when I return to put on canvas the brilliant, shimmering, and at once dramatic aspects of the *corrida* I attended' and to Astruc that he wanted to 'put on canvas the whole animated scene – the colourful multitude, and then the drama – the *picador* and his horse thrown down, mauled by the great horns, and the crowd of *chulos* trying to turn the enraged animal'. Manet probably painted this in his studio on his return, from sketches he had made on the spot. Here he visualizes the intentions he described in his letters. We see a large part of the arena with the climax of the bullfight and the stands, crowded with people in colourful dress, bathed in intense sunlight.

The Bullfight

Painted 1865–66
90 × 110cm
Musée d'Orsay, Paris

The Fifer was rejected from the Salon of 1866, and was the work which prompted Zola to write an article in *L'Evénement* in Manet's defence.

The work I like best is certainly The Fifer, *one of this year's Salon rejects. On a luminous grey background, the young musician stands forth, in undress uniform, red trousers with fatigue cap. He plays his instrument, full face and eyes front. I said before that M. Manet's talent lies in rightness and simplicity, and I was thinking especially of the impression this canvas left with me . . .*

This must have been an enormous encouragement to Manet, who had yet to sell a painting.

The young model who posed for the painting was a boy trooper in the Imperial Guard, introduced to Manet by his friend, Commandant Lejosne. He may have been inspired to paint a boy in uniform by popular prints, but he presents his subject without sentiment or superfluous detail. Manet had never been so bold in simplifying his technique. Japanese prints, highly popular at this time, influenced the broad flat areas of colour, the black outline of the trousers and the flatness of the background. A simple shadow is enough to stand the boy firmly on the ground. Manet's critics were startled by the lack of modelling. Daumier thought *The Fifer* was so flat that it resembled a playing card; another critic belittled the work by calling it an outfitter's signboard.

The Fifer

Painted 1866
161 × 97cm
Musée d'Orsay, Paris

This is Manet's first view of Paris, a great panorama seen from the Trocadero, from where many images of the city were taken for popular souvenir prints. He was inspired by the excitement of the World's Fair of 1867 which was the second of its kind to be held in Paris. These exhibitions were intended to promote the Second Empire and there were large international sections devoted to the arts. That year Manet decided not to present his work to the Salon jury but, instead, to hold an exhibition in a wooden shed, built at his own expense in the place de l'Alma. This was near the World's Fair in order to attract as many visitors as possible.

On the hill top Manet scattered figures from all walks of life. From left to right, there are a workman, two working-class women, a young girl and her companion, a couple of sightseers, a female on horseback, two street urchins, two fashionable dandies, three Imperial guardsmen and, in the foreground, Manet's adopted son, Léon Leenhoff, walking a dog. At the top right-hand corner Manet introduces the famous balloon of his photographer friend, Nadar.

View of the World's Fair

Painted 1867
108 × 196.5cm
Nasjonalgalleriet, Oslo

On 19 June 1867 the Emperor of Mexico, Max-imilian of Austria, was executed with Generals Miramon and Mejia. The French reacted with horror, at first against the Juarists in Mexico; but they then turned their anger on Napoleon III who, having made Maximilian Emperor, withdrew the French troops necessary to support him and left him to his fate at the hands of the Republic. The large scale of Manet's canvas suggests that he intended to create a major painting of a topical event for the Salon. He was evidently greatly involved in the subject and wanted to produce a painting of quality. He worked on four versions and a lithograph for more than a year, from immediately after the event to the end of 1868.

Manet painted the Mexican soldiers' uniform fol-lowing a description in *Le Figaro* which informed the reader that it was similar to that of the French. It was also known that Manet persuaded his friend, Com-mander Lejosne, to send soldiers to pose for him. It was thought that Manet's painting implied that French troops were the actual executioners – the authorities were horrified at the political implications and Manet was banned from exhibiting his works.

Although Manet used photographs of the Emperor and his Generals for their likenesses, the painting bears no similarity to the actual scene of execution. Manet had found a subject which allowed him to reinterpret a painting by one of the artists he most admired. Goya's *Third of May, 1808*, which he had seen in Madrid two summers before, obviously pro-vided inspiration for *The Execution of the Emperor Maximilian*. Manet's firing-squad, like Goya's, stand close to their victims, only a few paces apart in order to emphasize the horror of the event. Goya highlights his victim who throws out his arms in a gesture of despair (see page 29). Using cool greys and blacks, Manet's interpretation is relatively unemotional and detached. On the right, a soldier casually examines his gun, indifferent to the nearness of death. Renoir was reported to have said of this work, 'This is pure Goya, and yet Manet was never more himself'.

The Execution of the Emperor Maximilian

Painted 1867–68
252 × 305cm
Kunsthalle, Mannheim

The novelist and critic Emile Zola was one of the most vociferous defenders of Manet's work, and the value of his support for Manet and his contemporaries when they were under public attack cannot be underestimated. In 1866 Zola wrote an article praising Manet's works which had been rejected from the Salon of that year; Manet wrote to thank him, suggesting that they meet in the Café de Bade where he was to be found most evenings. Later in the year, Zola expanded the article, and published it in pamphlet form in 1867 to coincide with Manet's independent exhibition.

In appreciation of Zola's defence, Manet offered to paint his portrait. Zola recalled how in the long hours of sitting his motionless limbs would go numb. He is depicted, almost full-length, sitting informally at his desk. On the desk are books, the writer's quill pen and inkpot, his pipe and pamphlets, including the one he wrote on Manet. Although the setting is appropriate for the writer, the objects surrounding him are more representative of Manet than of Zola. The inkstand was apparently Zola's own, but the Japanese screen belonged to Manet and was one of the properties he had in his studio. The open book Zola is holding may be a volume of Charles Blanc's *L'Histoire des peintres*, one of the books which Manet owned and to which he most constantly referred. The frame on the upper right of the painting refers to Manet's career; a photograph of *Olympia*, a Japanese print and a reproduction of Velázquez's *The Drinkers*. The portrait was exhibited in the Salon of 1868 where critics reproached Manet for giving greater prominence to the accessories than to the sitter.

Emile Zola

Painted 1868
146 × 114cm
Musée d'Orsay, Paris

Manet met his future wife, Suzanne Leenhoff, when she was in her early twenties and gave piano lessons to his two younger brothers. Presumably Manet's father did not approve of their relationship as they lived together very discreetly for many years, and they did not marry until October 1863, a full year after his father's death. Manet must also have kept her secret from his friends, for Baudelaire wrote, 'Manet has just given me the most unexpected news. He's off to Holland tonight, and will return with *his bride*. There is some excuse for him though; it seems she's very beautiful, very nice, and a really good musician'.

Suzanne Leenhoff (1830–1906) was the daughter of a Dutch organist and was by all accounts an excellent pianist, especially of classical and modern German music, and Manet took great pleasure in hearing her play. In about 1865 Degas painted a portrait of Manet listening to his wife and gave it to him, but Manet disliked the depiction of Suzanne's face and, to Degas's fury, cut up the canvas. Manet may have been inspired by Degas to paint a version of his wife at the piano, in the salon of his mother's house at 49 rue de Saint-Petersbourg where they had been living for some months. The clock, according to Léon Leenhoff, would be the one given to Manet's mother by the King of Sweden, Charles XIV, at her wedding in 1831.

Madame Edouard Manet at the Piano

Painted 1867–68
38 × 46.5cm
Musée d'Orsay, Paris

*L*uncheon in the Studio is one of Manet's most ambiguous canvases. It was painted during the summer in Boulogne where he and his family had rented accommodation. The principal figure is the adolescent Léon Leenhoff, Suzanne's son and Manet's ward. To the right, smoking a cigar, is August Rousselin who was their neighbour in Boulogne and a former pupil of Couture's, at whose studio they had originally met.

The painting has a tension and demands an explanation for the gathering together of these figures. The boy with his boater could be leaving, and is perhaps anxious or irritated. Behind him, an unidentified maid either brings in or takes away a silver coffee-pot while the man remains indifferent. All this, however, is speculation, as if the painting were a scene from an unknown narrative. On the other hand, it has been suggested that the objects so carefully placed in the composition are symbols which would make the painting an allegory. What is the significance of the oysters and peeled lemon on the table, common features of Dutch seventeenth-century still lifes, and why is there armour on the chair to the left?

In 1869 *Luncheon in the Studio* was accepted at the Salon with *The Balcony*, and its painterly qualities, the subtle modulation of greys, and the still life were admired, although the naturalism of the subject matter was considered vulgar.

Luncheon in the Studio

Painted 1868
118 × 153.9cm
Neue Pinakothek, München

Manet is said to have had the idea for this painting during the summer of 1868 at Boulogne, when he noticed some figures on a balcony. The scene inspired him to reinterpret Goya's famous *Two Majas on a Balcony* and, once back from Boulogne, Manet asked friends to pose for him in his studio in the rue Guyot. The woman standing is Fanny Claus, a young concert violinist who saw a good deal of the Manets. Behind Fanny stands Antoine Guillemet, landscape painter, collector, and friend of the future Impressionists. Manet's future sister-in-law, Berthe Morisot, sits leaning on the decorative green rail of the balcony, and to the left, in half-darkness, the boy carrying the pitcher is Léon Leenhoff. They were all young, between the ages of twenty-two and twenty-seven, and complained about the long sittings.

The Balcony was accepted for the Salon of 1869 and Manet was nervous about its reception. Berthe Morisot recounts her visit to the Salon:

. . . I found Manet with a bewildered air. He begged me to go and look at his painting because he didn't dare put himself forward. I have never seen such an expressive face; he was laughing in an anxious way, at the same time insisting that his picture was very bad and that it was having a lot of success.

Again the public found Manet's painting disturbing and, indeed, it is a wonderfully haunting work. As in Goya's version, behind a balcony two women in light clothes stand out against a dark background. Goya's *Majas* are intimate; we witness them in conversation exchanging secrets. Manet's figures, however, do not communicate, each one absorbed in a world of his or her own.

The Balcony

Painted 1868–9
170 × 124.5cm
Musée d'Orsay, Paris

After the Franco-Prussian War, Manet left Paris to join his family in the South of France. The Parisians had surrendered after weeks of bombardment and then suffered the humiliation of their city's occupation by the German troops. The population opposed the newly-formed government which retreated to Versailles and a self-governing Commune was proclaimed in the capital. The Versaille government's troops attacked Paris and entered on 21 May. The following week was one of terror, known as *La semaine sanglante*, the week of blood, when 20,000 Parisians were killed.

Manet may have returned to Paris and witnessed the massacres at first hand but he would also have drawn on the many newspaper reports, prints and photographs which appeared. Manet's picture shows the execution of some Communards in front of a barricade. The grouping of the soldiers and their victims is reminiscent of *The Execution of the Emperor Maximilian* (page 87), and the similarity in composition may refer to the way Manet felt about these two terrible events. Manet owned a copy of Goya's series of etchings called *The Disasters of War*, from which he saw that a frank, detached account served to heighten the horror of an event.

Manet apparently experienced nervous depression after the war; his doctor was called in to treat him but it was not until the spring of 1872 that he was able to return to work seriously.

The Barricade

Drawn 1871
32.5 × 16.2cm
Budapest Museum of Fine Arts

One of Manet's constant visitors at his studio from the late 1860s was the painter Berthe Morisot, who had had some success with her work at the Salon. She had a profound respect for Manet's art but despite his protests she became one of the principal figures of Impressionism and an advocate of *plein air* painting. In 1898 George Moore said her works were 'the only pictures painted by a woman that could not be destroyed without creating a blank, a hiatus in the history of art'. In 1874 she married Eugène, Manet's brother, and Renoir had fond memories of the Manet house where he loved spending an hour or two in good company. 'Morisot acted like a special kind of magnet on people, attracting only the genuine. She had a gift for smoothing rough edges, even Degas became more civil with her'.

Morisot sat on several occasions for Manet. This is a rare example of Manet's portraiture where he depicts the sitter, not full or half-length in familiar surroundings, but close up, concentrating entirely on the face. This direct confrontation confirms the strong affection and artistic respect that these two friends had for each other.

Berthe Morisot
Painted 1872
55 × 38cm
Private Collection

One of the most significant developments of the Industrial Revolution was the advent of the steam train. Baron Haussmann's redevelopment of Paris included many new stations and the Gare Saint-Lazare, where Manet made sketches for this composition, was enlarged for the third time in the 1860s. The station was near the cafés frequented by Manet and his friends, and from it they journeyed up the Seine to the villages and coasts where they painted.

Manet was one of the first to take the railway station as a modern subject. Unlike Monet's series of pictures of trains entering the station, billowing smoke into the glass sheds, for Manet the steam of passing engines was a backdrop for a figure composition. The model for the woman was Victorine Meurent who reappeared ten years after posing for *Olympia*, having recently returned from America. The young girl was the daughter of a friend, Alphonse Hirsch, whose studio overlooked the Gare Saint-Lazare.

This was the only painting by Manet to be accepted for the Salon of 1873 and was, needless to say, ridiculed by the Press. They did not think the ordinary event of a child watching the trains go by while her guardian reads was an interesting subject. Where were the trains? The anxious passengers? The heroic engineer? It was instead retitled: 'Two sufferers from incurable Manet-mania watch the cars go by, through the bars of their madhouse'.

Gare Saint-Lazare

Painted 1872–3
93.3 × 114.5cm
National Gallery of Art, Washington DC

This painting was accepted by the Salon of 1873 and was Manet's first success since *The Spanish Singer* of 1861. It shows the engraver Emile Bellot sitting at a table in a café, enjoying a glass of beer and a pipe, and the public liked the simplicity of the subject. Manet had returned to popular old master styles and themes, particularly those of the Dutch school. He had recently made a study of the work of Frans Hals. As a result of this he received praise from critics who had previously shown only contempt for his work. It was probably due to this success that Manet refused to take part in his friends' 'independent' exhibition of 1874, during which they were labelled as Impressionists.

In spite of the dexterity it demonstrates, the image is bland and lacks Manet's usual incisive vision. The critic Albert Wolff recognized this and said that Manet had watered down his Bock. This prompted the reply from his friend, the artist Alfred Stevens, 'Some water? It's pure Haarlem beer'.

Due to a printing error, a periodical announced in June that a collector had offered 120,000 francs for *Le Bon Bock*. The editor only noticed the mistake when Manet appeared at the office, brandishing a copy of the article, and summoning him to name the madman willing to pay such a sum for his picture!

Le Bon Bock

Painted 1873
94 × 83cm
Philadelphia Museum of Art

*L*ady with Fans was the last of a number of paintings Manet executed of women reclining on a sofa. It is a portrait of Nina de Callias; a Baudelairean character, she was gifted and generous, known to be neurotic, temperamental, at times euphoric and at others depressed. She died aged thirty-nine driven insane by drink.

When Manet painted her she had one of the most exotic and brilliant literary and artistic salons in Paris. She attracted poets, musicians and painters and it was here that Manet probably met Mallarmé. She herself was an excellent pianist, composer and poet. Born Marie-Anne Gaillard, she took the more colourful name of her momentary husband, Hector de Callias, writer and journalist on *Le Figaro*. Manet painted her in his studio, surrounded by Japanese fans against which his contemporaries Whistler, Tissot, Renoir and Monet also set their female subjects. Manet was re-creating the decoration of the small town house where she lived, and she posed in one of the Algerian costumes in which she liked to receive her guests.

Lady with Fans

Painted 1873–74
113 × 166cm
Musée d'Orsay, Paris

Every year during Lent a famous masked ball was held at the Opéra. Paris was famous for the large number of theatres then active, their extravagant productions and brilliant performers. All classes of society attended and sat according to their means. Most modern novels of the time describe events at the theatre and Manet may also have been inspired by a scene at a masked ball in the Goncourt brothers' play *Henriette Marechal*.

Manet depicts the Opéra on rue le Peletier which was totally destroyed by fire in 1873 when he was still working on the painting; the present Opéra in Paris was still being built. For several months Manet went there to make sketches and, in his studio, recruited some of his male friends to form the groups of gentlemen in top hats. Manet himself appears, second figure from the right, with his blond beard: a card with his signature has fallen to the floor near his feet. The women are unidentified, flirting with the men in brightly coloured clothes, striped stockings and little lace-up shoes. Manet has used a frontal, horizontal composition as in *Music in the Tuileries Gardens* (page 63) to set the crowded, noisy, bustling scene of Parisian social life.

Masked Ball at the Opéra

Painted 1873–74
59 × 72.5cm
National Gallery of Art, Washington DC

Manet had decided not to participate in the independent exhibition, held in the spring of 1874, of the group who became known as the Impressionists. In spite of this and the fact that his interests differed radically from many of the principal artists of the group, especially Monet, he was still considered their leader in the eyes of the public. He was also very fond of Monet and helped him financially on several occasions. When the exhibition closed, Monet had difficulties paying his rent and Manet, through friends, found Monet a new house in Argenteuil. Subsequently, Manet decided to spend several weeks at his family's house at Gennevilliers, on the opposite banks of the Seine from Argenteuil.

During the summer Manet painted away from the studio, and encouraged by Monet, he worked *en plein air*. Influenced by the discoveries of the Impressionists he used brighter colours to capture the world out of doors and more descriptive brushwork. Here, the different strokes distinguish the bottom of a boat from the ripple of water or the vapour of smoke. Monet built this boat himself, from where, unaffected by the failure of the exhibition, he liked to watch the 'effects of light from one twilight to the next'. It is significant that, while Monet chose to paint the river and her banks, Manet was not inspired by the landscape and chose to paint his friend at work. Manet was primarily a figurative painter and, although this informal scene was conveniently before him, it is as if he wanted to record for posterity the way in which Monet worked, thereby paying homage to his friend's achievements.

Monet in his Floating Studio

Painted 1874
82.5 × 100.5cm
Neue Pinakothek, München

This painting evokes relaxed, idle summer afternoons spent on the banks of the Seine. Manet depicts an intimate scene, with a boatman and a girl sitting on a mooring dock with some sailing boats behind them. Across the blue Seine can be seen the houses and the small factory chimneys of Argenteuil.

Although the impression is an informal one, Manet has devised a structured composition of horizontals and verticals which makes the work more than merely a fleeting image of a scene captured by accident. He originally asked Monet and his wife to pose for him in their studio boat but he never finished the painting, probably due to the long sittings he required. Monet would surely have preferred to work on one of his own canvases than sit for others. Instead, Manet began a new canvas and asked models to come from Paris specifically for the composition. The woman in this painting has not been identified but the young man was Manet's brother-in-law, Rodolph Leenhoff. Together they sat for a work which depicts the private world of two people whose situation can only be guessed.

Argenteuil

Painted 1874
149 × 115cm
Musée des Beaux-Arts, Tournai

Many years after this picture was painted, Monet recollected that

Manet, enchanted by the colour and the light, had decided to do an open-air painting of people underneath the trees. While he was working, Renoir arrived. The charm of this hour appealed to him and he asked me for a palette, a brush and a canvas and there he was painting side by side with Manet. Manet watched him out of the corner of his eye and from time to time would approach the canvas. Then, with a kind of grimace, he passed discreetly close to me to whisper in my ear, pointing at Renoir: 'That boy has no talent . . . you're his friend, please tell him to give up painting!' Wasn't that amusing of Manet.

Manet's comment may have been made because he felt challenged by Renoir working beside him on the same motif, but it sounds more like it was made in jest, a flippant remark intended by Manet, the senior by nearly ten years, to make light of his alleged position as leader of the Impressionists. In the summer of 1874, the situation was quite the reverse and Manet learnt much from his Impressionist friends.

Manet's painting has an informal and relaxed atmosphere that shows no sign of a competitive spirit. It was painted rapidly to capture the charm of the scene; Camille Monet sitting under a tree, her son lying lazily on her lap while Monet tends to the garden. That summer, Manet, Monet and Renoir often painted together. They painted each other at work, *en plein air*, at their easels. Manet must have felt comfortable in the company of Monet and his family to be able to create one of his least confrontational figure groups.

The Monet Family in their Garden at Argenteuil

Painted 1874
61 × 99.7cm
The Metropolitan Museum of Art, New York

In September 1875 Manet and the painter James Tissot decided to go to Venice. Since fleeing the Commune in 1871, Tissot had been living in London. He planned to meet Manet and his wife in Paris and from there travel together to Venice. They cannot have stayed very long as by November Tissot was back in London.

In Venice, Manet met by chance the painter Charles Toché at the Café Florian in St. Mark's Square. Toché witnessed Manet working on his painting and recalled

I used to go and join him almost every day. The lagoon, the palaces, the old houses, scaled and mellowed by time, offered him an inexhaustible variety of subjects. I asked him if I might follow him in my gondola. 'As much as you like' he told me, 'When I am working, I pay no attention to anything but my subject.' . . .

I shall not forget Manet's enthusiasm for that motif; the white marble staircase against the faded pink bricks of the façade, and the cadmium and greens of the basements. Through the row of gigantic twisted posts, blue and white, one saw the domes of the incomparable Salute, dear to Guardi.

Toché implied that Manet did several views of Venice but only two, *The Grand Canal* and *Blue Venice*, exist today. Manet's 'enthusiasm for the motif' is evident as he describes the glorious intensity of Venetian colours with a medley of vivid brush-strokes.

The Grand Canal, Venice

Painted 1875
57 × 48cm
Private Collection

Mallarmé arrived in Paris in 1873 and probably met Manet in the salon of Nina de Caillias, when he was still an obscure poet. They were neighbours in the Batignolles quarter and soon became close friends. Mallarmé was very supportive of Manet and devoted two long articles to him in 1874, and an essay, 'The Impressionists and Edouard Manet', in the year this portrait was painted. After Manet's death Mallarmé lamented, 'I saw my dear Manet every day for ten years, and I find his absence today incredible'.

Manet painted Mallarmé in his studio in the rue Saint-Petersbourg in front of the same Japanese hanging seen in *Lady with Fans* and *Nana*. Mallarmé rests in the informal pose which Manet usually reserved for women; one of Mallarmé's pleasures was to talk to Manet while smoking a cigar. They were both admirers of Baudelaire, both enjoyed the company of women and both liked to dress elegantly. Mallarmé was devoted to the writing of Edgar Allan Poe and translated *The Raven* for which Manet made several illustrations. Manet also provided four drawings for Mallarmé's own poem, 'Prélude à l'après-midi d'un faune'. There are also portraits of Mallarmé by Gauguin, Edvard Munch, Renoir, and Whistler, but of these Manet's was considered unanimously to be the best likeness.

Stéphane Mallarmé

Painted 1876
27.5 × 35.9cm
Musée d'Orsay, Paris

Some fifteen years after *Olympia* Manet returned to the theme of the courtesan, this time without reference to an old master. In the late 1870s prostitution was highly topical in both literature and painting. The provocative character of Nana was introduced at the end of Zola's novel *L'Assommoir*, which was published in the autumn of 1876. Zola may have started his next book, in which Nana is the title and the heroine, while Manet worked on this painting. Zola's *Nana* tells the story of the success and downfall of a Parisian cocotte. Manet's painting shows her at the beginning of her career, with 'the fragrance of youth, the bare skin of child and of woman'. She is in complete control and entirely the centre of attention. As she turns to the spectator for confirmation of her charm, she seems to be deliberately keeping her patron waiting while she finishes her make-up and dresses at her leisure. He is cut off by the composition, implying that he is of little importance in spite of his smart evening clothes and the promises of a night at his expense.

Henriette Hauser, a young actress and popular boulevard figure, posed for Manet in front of the fashionable Japanese wall-hanging that was part of the decoration of his studio. With honesty and a touch of humour, Manet has painted a theme which was usually reserved for pornographic photography or caricature. He could have anticipated the scandal which followed. Predictably enough, *Nana* was rejected from the Salon on moral grounds. It was then exhibited in the window of a shop in the boulevard des Capucines where it reportedly caused riots, attracting crowds of people from morning to night who screamed with indignation.

Nana

Painted 1877
150 × 116cm
Kunsthalle, Hamburg

From 1872 until 1878 Manet had a studio on the second floor of 4 rue de Saint-Petersbourg (today rue de Leningrad) with a view down the newly laid-out rue Mosnier. In subject matter and style, *The Rue Mosnier with Pavers* has much in common with the paintings of his Impressionist friends. He describes the coming and going of a street he could watch at his leisure with seemingly rapid strokes of vivid colour.

Manet was a confirmed city-dweller and shows the street as a setting for human activity. In the foreground are road pavers, a common enough sight in Haussmann's new Paris which was, for years, a demolition and construction site. They are portrayed without sympathy for their toil. There are the new gas lamps. On the left is an advertisement for children's clothes, made to measure in the latest fashion. Behind the carriage on the right furniture is being moved. A few months after this canvas was painted, Zola described the street in his novel *Nana* as having 'fine houses, with narrow little apartments inhabited by ladies'. Perhaps, if Zola is to be believed, the black hackney carriages are waiting for the gentlemen who are taking their pleasure.

The Rue Mosnier with Pavers

Painted 1878
65.4 × 81.5cm
Private Collection

At the end of the eighteenth century the Café Maison de la Mère Moreau opened and became famous for serving plums soaked in brandy. By the mid-nineteenth century all cafés served them. In the opening of Zola's *L'Assommoir* a scene describes how eating and drinking these plums was a special treat for the working classes.

The café was an important part of Manet's social life but he did not paint its customers until the late 1870s. The setting of *The Plum* is described too vaguely to locate it specifically, but it has been suggested that it is the Café de la Nouvelle-Athènes, Manet's favourite café at the time. He probably constructed the scene in his studio with a model whose name is unknown. Degas also found this café a rich source of inspiration. His *Absinthe* was exhibited at the Impressionist exhibition of 1876 (see page 34) and a comparison reveals the entirely different atmosphere of these two paintings. Degas's figures sit alone, sunk in abject gloom which may only be numbed temporarily by the cheap drink. Manet's character, on the other hand, is ambiguous. She is lost in reverie and has forgotten to light her cigarette but she does not rely on the brandy-soaked plum for comfort. If she is a prostitute, she is not the ruined type Degas has depicted. She is more likely to be the type of young working-class woman who dressed above her station and frequented cafés as a place of idle entertainment.

The Plum

Painted 1878
73.6 × 50.2cm
National Gallery of Art, Washington DC

The setting for this urban 'slice of life' is the Cabaret de Reichshoffen, a popular café-concert on the boulevard of that name. The café-concert was a truly Parisian phenomenon; first appearing in the 1830s they became highly popular towards the end of the century. They were cafés which provided entertainment with singers, comic acts and acrobats. Some of the performers became famous and they could earn a considerable amount of money, but it was Degas who chose to concentrate on the celebrated figures of the day. In Manet's picture no-one is interested in the singer. She is relegated to the background and indeed is hardly visible. There is no interaction between the figures, no hint of emotion; they are caught in a world of their own, bound together only by circumstance. We are left to wonder what has caught the attention of the man with the top hat and we can only guess at what the figure on the left is thinking while she languidly smokes her cigarette.

At the Café

Painted 1878
47.5 × 30.3cm
The Walters Art Gallery, Baltimore

In most of Manet's café scenes, he invites us to be a casual, objective observer of the lower-class customers of popular haunts in Paris. Here, however, he presents us with a woman whose stylish dress suggests more affluent means. She is engrossed in an illustrated periodical borrowed from the café's reading-rack. She may be reading something similar in kind to *La Vie Moderne*, the recently inaugurated chronicle of artistic, social and literary life in Paris. She is completely content with her surroundings, a glass of beer at her side, and her animated face conveys that she is intelligently amused by what she is reading. The background is indiscernable, the figure all-important. Manet probably arranged the composition and model in his studio and he has applied vibrant colour with vigorous brushwork, as if he wanted to record quickly an enjoyable but fleeting image.

Le Journal Illustré

Painted 1879
61.7 × 50.7cm
The Art Institute of Chicago

George Moore was an Anglo-Irishman of some means who came to Paris in 1873 with the intention of becoming a painter. He started to study under Cabanel but gave up a few years later and, to Degas's horror, turned to art criticism. He had a studio at the foot of Montmartre and became a frequenter of the Café de la Nouvelle-Athènes. Here he met Zola, Manet and the many other habitués of the Café. It was George Moore who gave us the most vivid description of the Café and its customers.

Although Moore was described as a golden-haired fop, an aesthete before the days of Oscar Wilde, he was welcomed everywhere because his manners were amusing and his French very funny. Manet painted him three times, here in pastel which gives the portrait a fresh, spontaneous appearance. It also allowed him to execute the portrait in a single sitting, something Manet was rarely able to do. Manet made about ninety works in pastel but the large majority of these were portraits of women. Perhaps Manet chose pastel as the most effective way to portray George Moore's somewhat eccentric appearance. Initially, Moore was dissatisfied with his image, and Manet recounted, 'He came bothering me, wanting a change here, an alteration there. I won't change a thing. Is it my fault that Moore has that look of a broken egg-yolk, or if the sides of his face are not aligned'. Manet's portrait was described by the critics as 'the drowned man taken out of the water', and the sitter must have had curious features for his portrait by Blanche made him 'look like a drunken cabby' while Sickert's version was called 'an intoxicated mummy', 'a boiled ghost' and 'a leprous portrait'. Moore must have preferred Manet's portrait as he chose it for the frontispiece of his volume of collected essays, entitled *Modern Painting*, of 1893.

George Moore

Painted 1879
55.2 × 35.2cm
The Metropolitan Museum of Art, New York

At intermittent stages of Manet's career he painted the female nude; this is one of four pastels he executed of women at their toilet. Manet chose pastel because the sketch-like, spontaneous effect of the medium is entirely in accord with the intimacy of the scene. Informal images of women at their toilet were most extensively depicted by Degas and became yet another cause for rivalry between the two artists. However, Degas's famous nudes of ordinary women getting in or out of the tub, combing their hair or drying it, were done after Manet's death.

While Degas's women are preoccupied, seen 'as if you looked through a keyhole', Manet's nude has been interrupted, and is aware but unafraid of the spectator. She is uninhibited, involved in the simple task of washing herself. It is as if Manet asked her to hold a pose he saw by accident in order to create this extremely informal scene.

The Bath

Painted 1878–79
55 × 45cm
Musée d'Orsay, Paris

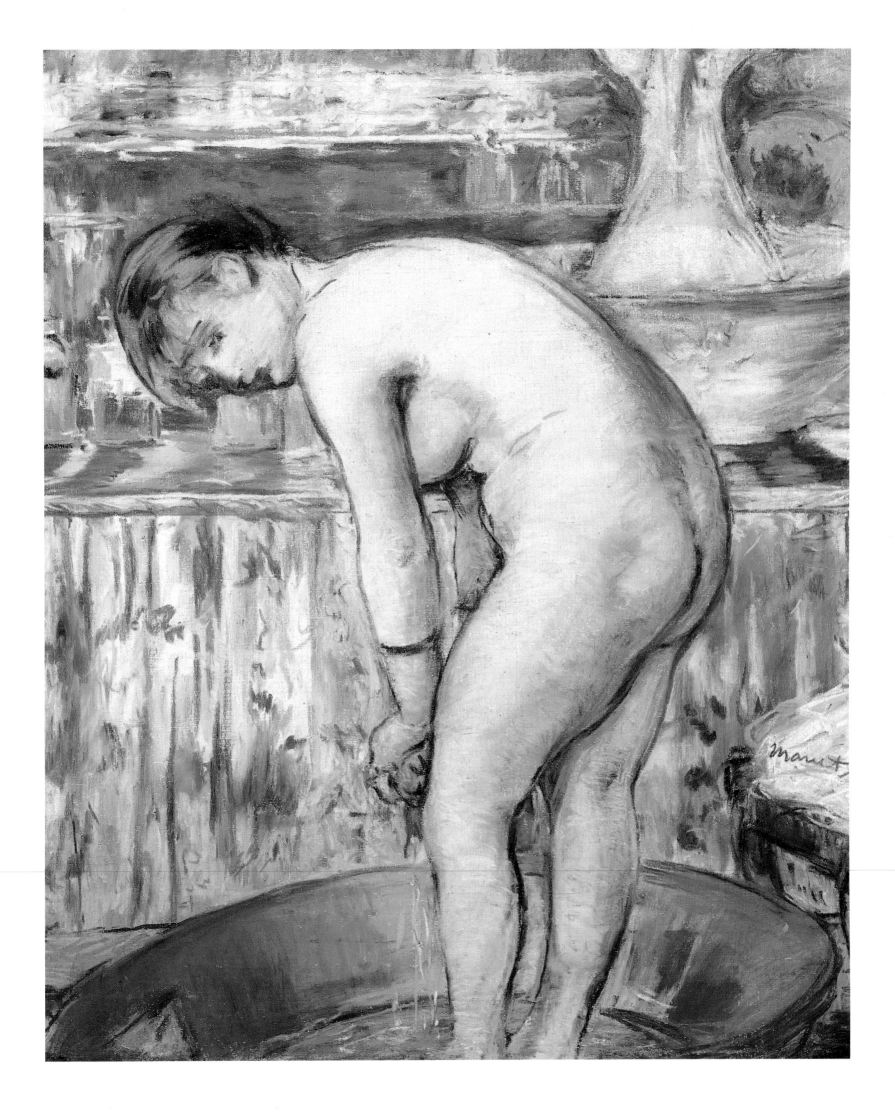

Manet and Antonin Proust had known each other since childhood; they were fellow pupils at the College Rollin and were close friends throughout their lives. Proust recounted this long friendship at the end of Manet's life in a series of articles which were later revised and published as his memoirs in 1913. They are the key if not always reliable source of information about Manet's career and personality.

Proust was a journalist, critic and successful politician. During the Franco-Prussian War he acted as Minister of the Interior and was responsible for the refugees who were pouring into the city. Ten years later, when this portrait was executed, he briefly held the position of Minister of Fine Arts. In spite of the short time in which he held this post, he managed to obtain the award of the Légion d'honneur for Manet. Because of the formality of the portrait, compared to that of Zola, Mallarmé and other close friends, with hand on hip, gloves and cane, top hat and smart clothes, Manet was accused of ingratiating himself with his influential friend. The image has, however, a dignity appropriate to Proust's public position. Proust genuinely admired the work of his friend. In 1884 he was one of the organizers of a memorial exhibition in honour of Manet at the Ecole des Beaux-Arts, and gave an oration at the banquet held by Manet's family and friends to celebrate the event.

Antonin Proust

Painted 1880
129.5 × 95.9cm
The Toledo Museum of Art, Toledo, Ohio

When Manet painted this sketch, Henri Roche-fort was the romantic hero of a dramatic escape from prison. He stood for patriotic Republicanism; during the Second Empire he had founded *La Lantern*, in which he voiced his ardent views against the Imperial regime and Napoleon III. Rochefort was active in the Commune and was deported in 1873. He escaped from the penal colony of Nouméa in New Caledonia in 1874, returning to Paris on 21 July 1880 under an amnesty. Manet might have met him at the salon of Nina de Callias, which Rochefort frequented, and they would also have known each other through the painter and etcher, Marcellin Desboutin, who was Rochefort's relative. Manet asked him for full details of the escape, which had happened six years previously, and Desboutin acted as intermediary. Manet could also have drawn on a description which Rochefort published some months before the painting was executed. Rochefort had escaped with four companions in a whale-boat; an Australian ship was waiting for them and put them ashore in the United States. For dramatic and pictorial reasons Manet deviated from the actual events. The escape had happened at night and the boat which picked up the men was, in fact, in the sheltered waters of a harbour, not on the high seas Manet has chosen to depict in order to express the precariousness of their situation.

Like *The Battle of the* Kearsage *and the* Alabama (page 75), Manet chose to paint a current event which happened at sea for the Salon. However, he submitted neither of the two versions he executed. By this time Manet was ill, although he was able to continue to work seriously and had a model of the boat carried into his garden in the rue d'Amsterdam. This theme must have reminded him of the past and one of Manet's favourite subjects of conversation was the time of his travels – to Cherbourg, to Italy and Spain and especially to the seaside.

The Escape of Rochefort

Painted 1880–81
146 × 116cm
Kunsthaus, Zürich

A *Bar at the Folies-Bergère* is a summary of the experience of a life-time, painted when Manet was too weak to stand without a stick. Manet went to the Folies-Bergère, one of the most fashionable café-concerts in Paris, to make quick sketches on the spot and the final composition was arranged in his studio. His subject is the barmaid, not the stars, the trapeze artists or performers whom Degas chose to paint. He asked Suzon, a girl who actually worked at the bar, to pose for him. He set her behind a marble top laden with bottles of champagne, *crème de menthe*, and Bass Charrington's beer with its red triangle on the label. By chance, the drinks are all still recognizable today, which makes the painting even more accessible. As for many of his other works, Manet asked friends to pose for him. The man with the top hat is the painter Gaston La Touche and, in the background, Méry Laurent posed for the woman in a white dress, her elbows on the balcony, wearing yellow gloves. The figure immediately behind her in a box is the young actress Jeanne Demarsy.

Behind the serving-girl is what seems to be a gilt-edged mirror reflecting figures seated in the circle of the auditorium opposite, under the great chandelier. They ignore the trapeze act in mid-performance, cut off by the canvas, but we can see her green-clad feet at the top left. If it is a mirror behind the barmaid, the reflections are illogical – the bottles appear on the wrong edge of the bar. In the reflection the barmaid is in close proximity to, and appears intimate with, the man. The girl we are facing is detached and set further back. These discrepancies may be the result of substantial changes Manet made while he was painting, which can be seen in X-ray photographs. In spite of their disagreements, Manet would share Degas's view that 'Art is deceit . . . A painting requires a certain mystery, something undefined'. Perspective in painting, correct or incorrect, is artificial. Manet's description of a bustling bar is an extremely potent image of an entirely urban situation.

A Bar at the Folies-Bergère

Painted 1881–82
96 × 130cm
Courtauld Institute Galleries, London

Manet spent his last summer in a house he had rented at Rueil-Malmaison, just outside Paris. The previous year he had heeded his doctor's advice, taking a rest in the countryside in order to fight the illness attacking the nervous system that had afflicted him since 1879. By 1882 he could only walk with a cane and was forced to remain seated most of the time. In the summer of 1874 Manet had enjoyed painting *en plein air* with Monet and Renoir but at Rueil he felt that he had been banished to the countryside and that landscape had charm only for those who were not forced to stay there.

Manet sat in the shade of the tree to paint the garden front of the house and the result gives no hint that he was suffering pain and was frustrated by his disabilities. *The House at Rueil* is a rare example of a work by Manet which contains no human figures, although the bench and open door and windows suggest that the house is occupied. It is Impressionist in approach, painted with a great variety of brush-strokes and with strong contrasts of light and shade. But in Manet's paintings there is always a structure to the composition, here clearly defined by the horizontals and verticals of the house and tree. During the following months Manet was only able to paint flowers; his last work is of a bunch of lilacs and roses arranged in a Japanese vase.

The House at Rueil

Painted 1882
92 × 72.5cm
Berlin, Statliche Museen

CHRONOLOGY

1832
Manet born 23 January at 5 rue des Petits-Augustins, Paris.
1839
Attends school of Canon Poiloup as day-boy.
1842
Studies at College Rollin where he meets Antonin Proust.
1848
Fails entrance exams to the Navy.
Goes to sea as an apprentice-cadet on *Le Havre et Guadeloupe*.
1849
In Rio de Janeiro.
In July finally rejected for the Navy. Meets future wife, Suzanne Leenhoff, in Paris.
1850
Enters Couture's studio.
1851
Birth of Léon-Edouard Leenhoff, son of Suzanne Leenhoff.
1852
First trip to Netherlands; name appears on register of the Rijksmuseum, Amsterdam.
1853
Trip to Dresden, Prague, Vienna and Munich.
In September visits Italy with brother Eugène.
1855
Visits Delacroix.
World's Fair held in Paris.
1856
Leaves Couture's studio.
Rents a studio on rue Lavoisier.
1857
Meets Fantin-Latour.
Travels to Germany and Italy.
1859
The Absinthe Drinker is rejected by the Salon.
Moves to a studio on rue de la Victoire.
Meets Degas at the Louvre.
1860
Establishes a studio on rue de Douai and rents an apartment on rue de l'Hotel de Ville in the Batignolles quarter, with Suzanne and Léon.
1861
The Spanish Singer is accepted by the Salon.
Establishes a studio at 81 rue Guyot.
1862
Exhibits several etchings with the Société des Aquafortistes of which he is a founder member.
Frequents the Café Tortoni.

Meets model Victorine Meurent.
Father dies, leaving Manet with a substantial inheritance.
1863
Exhibition at Martinet's Gallery of fourteen paintings, including *Music in the Tuileries Gardens*.
At the Salon des Refusés exhibits *Le déjeuner sur l'herbe*.
Attends Delacroix's funeral in August.
Marries Suzanne Leenhoff.
1864
Episode from a Bullfight and *Dead Christ with Angels* accepted by the Salon.
Moves into an apartment at 34 boulevard des Batignolles.
Paints scenes at the racecourse.
1865
Olympia accepted by the Salon.
Exhibits nine canvases at Martinet's Gallery.
Visits Spain for two weeks in August.
Begins frequenting the Café Guerbois with other artists.
1866
Exhibits *The Fifer* and *The Tragic Actor* in his studio after their rejection by the Salon.
Zola writes an article in defence of Manet in *L'Evénement*.
Meets Zola, Monet and Cézanne.
Moves to live with Mme Manet at 49 rue de Saint-Petersbourg.
1867
Zola publishes a twenty-three page defence of Manet in *L'Artiste; Revue du XIX Siecle*.
Paris World's Fair; Manet erects his own pavilion and exhibits fifty paintings.
Forbidden to show *The Execution of the Emperor Maximilian*.
Spends summer at Boulogne and Trouville.
Funeral of Baudelaire.
1868
Portrait of Emile Zola accepted by the Salon.
Spends summer in Boulogne.
Berthe Morisot begins to frequent his studio.
1869
Eva Gonzalès poses for him and becomes his pupil.
The Balcony accepted at the Salon.
Spends summer in Boulogne.
Duel takes place between Manet and Duranty.
1870
Franco-Prussian War.
Sends family to Oloron-Sainte-Marie, in the Pyrenees.
In November enlists in the National Guard with rank of lieutenant.
1871
Joins his family in the country.
Possibly witnesses the end of the Paris Commune.

Spends summer in Boulogne.

La Nouvelle-Athènes replaces Guerbois as artists' rendezvous.

1872

Paul Durand-Ruel buys twenty-four canvases.

Battle of the Kearsage *and the* Alabama exhibited at the Salon.

Travels to Holland; admires Hals and Jongkind.

Moves to a new studio on the rue de Saint-Petersbourg.

1873

Exhibits *Le Repos* and *Le Bon Bock* at the Salon.

Beginning of friendship with Mallarmé.

Spends summer at Etaples.

1874

The Railroad accepted by the Salon.

Mallarmé writes a defence of two rejected works.

Exhibition of Société Anonyme des artistes, peintres, sculpteurs, graveurs opens in April, at Nadar's on the boulevard des Capucines; Manet takes no part.

Spends summer at Gennevilliers; works with Monet at Argenteuil.

Marriage of Eugène Manet and Berthe Morisot.

1875

Illustrates Mallarmé's translation of Edgar Allan Poe's *The Raven*.

Argenteuil exhibited at the Salon.

Travels to Venice with Tissot; paints the canals.

1876

Mallarmé's poem 'Prélude à l'après-midi d'un faune' published, with wood engravings by Manet.

Holds an exhibition in his studio to show works including those rejected that year by the Salon; Méry Laurent is among the many visitors.

Spends August in Normandy.

1877

The Tragic Actor accepted by the Salon; *Nana* is rejected.

1878

Auction of belongings of the collector Hoschedé is an utter failure; Manet's paintings fetch nothing.

Evicted from studio for having held a public exhibition; moves to the rue d'Amsterdam.

1879

Offers to decorate the Hotel de Ville with paintings of contemporary Parisian scenes.

Falls ill in September; rest and treatment at Bellevue.

1880

Exhibits in the offices of *La Vie Moderne*. *Portrait of Antonin Proust* shown at the Salon.

Rents house at Bellevue for a rest cure; onset of fatal illness.

1881

Exhibits *Portrait of Rochefort* at the Salon, which receives a second class medal.

Rents a summer villa at Versailles for treatment.

Antonin Proust becomes Minister of Fine Arts.

Elected a Chevalier de la Légion d'honneur.

1882

A Bar at the Folies-Bergère exhibited at the Salon.

Spends summer at Rueil.

Great difficulty in walking.

1883

In April loses use of his legs and is bedridden.

Left leg is amputated 20 April; operation unsuccessful.

Dies 30 April.

Buried in Passy cemetery on 3 May.

1884

Posthumous exhibition of works held at the Ecole des Beaux-Arts.

SELECTED BIBLIOGRAPHY

CLARK, T.J., *The Painting of Modern Life: Paris and the art of Manet and his followers*, London, 1985.

COURTHION, Pierre, and CAILLER, Pierre (eds.), *Portrait of Manet by himself and his contemporaries*, Geneva, 1953; translation by Michael Ross, London, 1960.

DENVIR, Bernard, *The Encyclopedia of Impressionism*, London, 1990.

HANSON, Anne Coffin, *Manet and the Modern Tradition*, Yale, 1977.

PROUST, Antonin, *Edouard Manet, Souvenirs*, Paris, 1913.

REFF, Theodore, *Manet and Modern Paris: One Hundred Paintings, Drawings, Prints and Photographs by Manet and his followers*, Chicago, 1982.

REWALD, John, *The History of Impressionism*, New York, 1946.

WILSON-BAREAU, Juliet, *Manet by himself*, London, 1991.

EXHIBITION CATALOGUES

Edouard Manet 1832–1883, Gallerie National du Grand Palais, Paris and The Metropolitan Museum of Art, New York, 1983.

Manet at Work: Exhibition to mark the centenary of the death of Edouard Manet 1832–1883, National Gallery, London, 1983.

LIST OF PLATES

All paintings are by Manet unless otherwise identified.

7 *The Absinthe Drinker*, 1858–59. Oil on canvas, 117.5 × 103 cm. NY Carlsberg Glyptotek, Copenhagen.

9 Edgar Degas, *Study for a Portrait of Edouard Manet*, *c.*1864. Black chalk and estompe, 32.5 × 22.8 cm. All rights reserved, The Metropolitan Museum of Art, Rogers Fund, 1918.

12 *Baudelaire wearing a hat*, 1867–1868. Etching, first state, 10.9 × 9 cm. Bibliothèque Nationale, Paris.

15 Giorgione, *Fête Champêtre*, *c.*1510. Oil on canvas, 105 × 136.5 cm. Musée du Louvre, Paris. © Photo: RMN.

16 Marcantonio Raimondi, *The Judgement of Paris*. Engraving after Raphael. All rights reserved, The Metropolitan Museum of Art, Rogers Fund, 1919.

17 Alexandre Cabanel, *The Birth of Venus, c.*1863. Oil on canvas, 130 × 225 cm. Musée d'Orsay, Paris. © Photo: RMN.

19 Titian, *Venus of Urbino*, 1538. Oil on wood, 117.5 × 162.5 cm. Galleria degli Uffizi, Florence.

21 Kitigaro Utamaro, *Two courtesans, One Reading a Letter and the Other Playing the Samisen*, late eighteenth century. 'Ukiyo-e' woodblock colour print, 32.1 × 19.1 cm. Victoria and Albert Museum, London.

22 *The Balloon*, 1862. Lithograph, 39.5 × 51 cm. S P Avery Collection, Miriam and Ira D Wallach Division of Art, Prints and Photographs, The New York Public Library; Astor, Lenox and Tilden Foundations.

25 *A Café Interior (The Café Guerbois)*, 1869. Pen and black ink on pale tan paper, 29.5 × 39.5 cm. Courtesy of the Fogg Art Museum, Harvard University, Cambridge, Massachusetts. Bequest of Meta and Paul J Sachs.

26 Bertall, *Jesus Painting among his Disciples or 'The Divine School of Manet' religious picture by Fantin-Latour*. Caricature.

27 Henri Fantin-Latour, *A Studio in the Batignolles Quarter*, 1870. Oil on canvas, 204 × 273.5 cm. Musée d'Orsay, Paris. © Photo: RMN.

28 Claude Monet, *Le déjeuner sur l'herbe*, 1865–66. Oil on canvas, 130 × 181 cm. Pushkin Museum, Moscow. Photo: The Bridgeman Art Library.

29 Francisco de Goya, *The Third of May, 1808*, 1814. Oil on canvas, 266 × 345 cm. Museo del Prado, Madrid.

30 Francisco de Goya, *Two Majas on a Balcony*, 1800–12. Oil on canvas, 194.8 × 125.7 cm. All rights reserved, The Metropolitan Museum of Art.

34 Edgar Degas, *Absinthe*, 1876. Oil on canvas, 92 × 68 cm. Musée d'Orsay, Paris. © Photo: RMN.

35 'The Chair', illustration from *The Raven*, 1875. Lithograph. Photo: © The British Library.

37 *Eva Gonzalès*, 1870. Oil on canvas, 191 × 133 cm. Reproduced by courtesy of the Trustees, The National Gallery, London.

38 *Isabelle Diving*, 1880. Watercolour, 20 × 12.3 cm. Musée du Louvre, Cabinet des Dessins, Paris. © Photo: RMN.

39 *A Café, Place du Théâtre Français, c.*1877–78. Pastel on canvas, 32.4 × 45.7 cm. The Burrell Collection, Glasgow Museums.

41 Paul Cézanne, *A Modern Olympia, c.*1873. Oil on canvas, 46 × 55.5 cm. Musée d'Orsay, Paris. © Photo: RMN.

42 Nadar, Photograph of Edouard Manet, *c.*1865. Photo: Bibliothèque Nationale, Paris.

45 *The Spanish Singer*, 1860. Oil on canvas, 147.3 × 114.3 cm. All rights reserved, The Metropolitan Museum of Art, Gift of William Church Osborn, 1949.

47 *Boy with a Sword*, 1861. Oil on canvas, 131.1 × 93.3 cm. All rights reserved, The Metropolitan Museum of Art, Gift of Erwin Davis, 1889.

49 *The Surprised Nymph*, 1859–61. Oil on canvas, 144.5 × 112.5 cm. Museo Nacional de Bellas Artes, Buenos Aires.

51 *The Old Musician*, 1861–62. Oil on canvas, 187.4 × 248.3 cm. National Gallery of Art, Washington DC; Chester Dale Collection.

53 *Baudelaire's Mistress, Reclining*, 1862. Oil on canvas, 90 × 113 cm. Reproduced by courtesy of the Board of Directors of the Budapest Museum of Fine Arts.

55 *Young Woman Reclining in Spanish Costume*, 1862. Oil on canvas, 94 × 113 cm. Yale University Art Gallery, Bequest of Stephen Carlton Clark, BA 1903.

57 *Mademoiselle Victorine in the Costume of an Espada*, 1862. Oil on canvas, 165.1 × 127.6 cm. All rights reserved, The Metropolitan Museum of Art, Bequest of Mrs H O Havemeyer, 1929. The H O Havemeyer Collection.

59 *Lola de Valence*, 1862. Oil on canvas, 123 × 92 cm. Musée d'Orsay, Paris. © Photo: RMN.

61 *The Street Singer*, c.1862. Oil on canvas, 171.3 × 105.8 cm. Courtesy, Museum of Fine Arts, Boston, Bequest of Sarah Choate Sears in Memory of her husband, Joshua Montgomery Sears.

63 *Music in the Tuileries Gardens*, 1862. Oil on canvas, 76.2 × 118.1 cm. Reproduced by courtesy of the Trustees, The National Gallery, London.

65 *Le déjeuner sur l'herbe*, 1863. Oil on canvas, 208 × 264.5 cm. Musée d'Orsay, Paris. © Photo: RMN.

67 *Olympia*, 1863. Oil on canvas, 130.5 × 190 cm. Musée d'Orsay, Paris. © Photo: RMN.

69 *The Dead Toreador*, 1864. Oil on canvas, 75.9 × 153.3 cm. National Gallery of Art, Washington DC; Widener Collection.

71 *The Dead Christ with Angels*, 1864. Oil on canvas, 179.4 × 149.9 cm. All rights reserved, The Metropolitan Museum of Art, Bequest of Mrs H O Havemeyer, 1929. The H O Havemeyer Collection.

73 *Vase of Peonies*, 1864. Oil on canvas, 93.2 × 70.2 cm. Musée d'Orsay, Paris. © Photo: RMN.

75 *The Battle of the* Kearsage *and the* Alabama, 1864. Oil on canvas, 145 × 130 cm. Philadelphia Museum of Art: The John G Johnson Collection.

77 *Races at Longchamp*, 1864. Oil on canvas, 43.9 × 84.5 cm. Mr and Mrs Potter Palmer Collection, 1922.424. Photo: © 1991, The Art Institute of Chicago. All rights reserved.

79 *The Tragic Actor (Rouvière as Hamlet)*, 1865–66. Oil on canvas, 187.2 × 108.1 cm. National Gallery of Art, Washington; Gift of Edith Stuyvesant Gerry.

81 *The Bullfight*, c.1865–66. Oil on canvas, 90 × 110.5 cm. Musée d'Orsay, Paris. © Photo: RMN.

83 *The Fifer*, 1866. Oil on canvas, 161 × 97 cm. Musée d'Orsay, Paris. © Photo: RMN.

85 *View of the World's Fair*, 1867. Oil on canvas, 108 × 196.5 cm. © Nasjonalgalleriet, Oslo. Photo: Jacques Lathion.

87 *The Execution of the Emperor Maximilian*, 1867–68. Oil on canvas, 252 × 305 cm. Kunsthalle, Mannheim.

89 *Emile Zola*, 1868. Oil on canvas, 146 × 114 cm. Musée d'Orsay, Paris. © Photo: RMN.

91 *Madame Manet at the Piano*, 1867–68. Oil on canvas, 38 × 46.5 cm. Musée d'Orsay, Paris. © Photo: RMN.

93 *Luncheon in the Studio*, 1868. Oil on canvas, 118 × 153.9 cm. Neue Pinakothek, München. Photo: Artothek.

95 *The Balcony*, 1868–69. Oil on canvas, 170 × 124.5 cm. Musée d'Orsay, Paris. © Photo: RMN.

97 *The Barricade*, 1871. Pencil, ink wash, watercolour and gouache, 32.5 × 16.2 cm. Reproduced by courtesy of the Board of Directors of the Budapest Museum of the Fine Arts.

99 *Berthe Morisot (with a bouquet of violets)*, 1872. Oil on canvas, 55 × 38 cm. Private Collection. © Photo: RMN.

101 *Gare Saint-Lazare (The Railway)*, 1873. Oil on canvas,

93.3 × 114.5 cm. National Gallery of Art, Washington DC; Gift of Horace Havemeyer in memory of his mother, Louisine W Havemeyer.

103 *Le Bon Bock*, 1873. Oil on canvas, 94 × 83 cm. Philadelphia Museum of Art: The Mr and Mrs Carroll S Tyson Collection.

105 *Lady with Fans (Portrait of Nina de Callias)*, 1873–74. Oil on canvas, 113 × 166 cm. Musée d'Orsay, Paris. © Photo: RMN.

107 *Masked Ball at the Opéra*, 1873. Oil on canvas, 59 × 72.5 cm. National Gallery of Art, Washington; Gift of Mrs Horace Havemeyer in memory of her mother-in-law, Louisine W Havemeyer.

109 *Monet in his Floating Studio*, 1874. Oil on canvas, 82.5 × 100.5 cm. Neue Pinakothek, München. Photo: Artothek.

111 *Argenteuil*, 1874. Oil on canvas, 149 × 115 cm. Musée des Beaux-Arts, Tournai. Photo: Giraudon.

113 *The Monet Family in their Garden at Argenteuil*, 1874. Oil on canvas, 61 × 99.7 cm. All rights reserved, The Metropolitan Museum of Art, Bequest of Joan Whitney Payson, 1975.

115 *The Grand Canal, Venice*, 1875. Oil on canvas, 57 × 48 cm. Private Collection.

117 *Stéphane Mallarmé*, 1876. Oil on canvas, 27.5 × 36 cm. Musée d'Orsay, Paris. © Photo: RMN.

119 *Nana*, 1877. Oil on canvas, 150 × 116 cm. Kunsthalle, Hamburg.

121 *The rue Mosnier with Pavers*, 1878. Oil on canvas, 65.4 × 81.5 cm. Private Collection.

123 *The Plum*, 1878. Oil on canvas, 73.6 × 50.2 cm. National Gallery of Art, Washington DC; Collection of Mr and Mrs Paul Mellon.

125 *At the Café*, 1878. Oil on canvas, 47.5 × 30.3 cm. The Walters Art Gallery, Baltimore.

127 *Le Journal Illustré*, c.1878–79. Oil on canvas, 61.2 × 50.7 cm. Mr and Mrs Lewis Larned Coburn Memorial Collection, 1933.435. Photo: © 1991. The Art Institute of Chicago. All rights reserved.

129 *George Moore*, 1879. Pastel on fine canvas, 55.3 × 35.3 cm. The Metropolitan Museum of Art, Bequest of Mrs H O Havemeyer, 1929. The H O Havemeyer Collection.

131 *The Bath*, 1878–79. Pastel on board, 55 × 45 cm. Musée d'Orsay, Paris. © Photo: RMN.

133 *Antonin Proust*, 1880. Oil on canvas, 129.5 × 95.9 cm. The Toledo Museum of Art, Toledo, Ohio; Gift of Edward Drummond Libbey.

135 *The Escape of Rochefort*, 1880–81. Oil on canvas, 146 × 116 cm. Kunsthaus, Zürich.

137 *A Bar at the Folies-Bergère*, 1881–82. Oil on canvas, 96 × 130 cm. Courtauld Institute Galleries, London. Courtauld Gift 1934.

139 *The House at Rueil*, 1882. Oil on canvas, 92 × 72.5 cm. Staatliche Museen Preussischer Kulturbesitz, Nationalgalerie, Berlin.